HOP OFF
THE BANDWAGON.

Stand apart in Genuine™ Harley-Davidson® MotorClothes® and leave the trendsetters behind. These styles look great on and off the road and are based on tradition, not trends. MotorClothes are only available at your authorized Harley-Davidson dealer. See the selection today and pull ahead of the bandwagon.

*Genuine™ Harley-Davidson®
MotorClothes®*

FOR A GENUINE HARLEY-DAVIDSON DEALER NEAR YOU,
PLEASE SEE PAGES **92 & 93**

© 1995, H-D

Southern California Harley-Davidson Dealers'

MOTORCYCLE TOURING
IN SOUTHERN CALIFORNIA

written by
Jan Williams and Judith B. Uthus

edited by
Mark Blocker

Motorcycle Touring in Southern California

Fifth Edition 2000
First Edition 1996
Copyright 1994

Published by
Black Ball Publishing
Calabasas, CA
(818) 224-3782

Printed in Canada

INTRODUCTION

All dressed in leather with no place to go? Whether you're in the mood for conquering corkscrew turns on 70-degree inclines or for riding into a desert sunset, the *Southern California Harley-Davidson Dealers' Motorcycle Touring in Southern California* knows just what riders want. Inside these pages motorcycle pros share with you the best pavement and sights of Southern California.

Motorcycle Touring in Southern California describes the highlights of the road via iron horse; riding terrain, pavement condition, weather exposure, biker friendly stops, scenery, and sightseeing ideas that all cater to two-wheel touring. You'll discover the best roads in Southern California whether you just bought your bike or rode with the Hell's Angels to Altamont. Our riding experts will introduce you to new places, link roads that offer riding variety, and provide area highlights. Riding skill and sport interest levels are incorporated into every chapter. If you're looking for the area's tightest hairpin turns, you'll locate them inside these pages. If you want to avoid a "crotch rocket pocket," this guide will tell you just where they are. You'll discover what it really means to go joy riding, every time you hop in the saddle.

Each tour is illustrated so you can easily map roads and locate biker hangouts, restaurants, fuel stops, and hotel accommodations. Appendices list motorcycle hot spots and where to get more information on an area. Factory-authorized Harley-Davidson dealers are listed to help outfit you or your bike with all riding needs from service, sales, and parts to riding attire and gifts. Visit the 26 shops throughout Southern California to discover the wide range of Genuine Harley-Davidson merchandise available for you and your friends.

With its weather and riding opportunities, there's not a better place in the world to own a bike than Southern California. Take advantage of these writers' and riders' expertise by keeping a copy of *Southern California Harley-Davidson Dealers' Motorcycle Touring in Southern California* under your saddle. Happy Trails!

ABOUT THE CONTRIBUTORS...

JAN WILLIAMS is a Harley-Davidson customer service representative who has covered just about every portion of pavement in Southern California. Her ability to intimately describe the countryside as well as road conditions benefit those who use this book. She also organizes and leads group riding tours. Jan is not the average grandmother, clocking at least 16,000 miles each year on her Harley Sportster with husband Mickey at her side.

LARRY LANE who is a native of California has been in the saddle since 1959. He was a Desert Rider and a "Hare and Hound" racing competitor throughout the Southwest. Larry has ridden all brands of bikes, and currently owns a Harley 1995 Electra Glide Standard and a 1994 Road King that clock at least 20,000 miles a year. His favorite travelling companion is his better half, Mary Voigt.

JUDITH B. UTHUS confesses she's only ridden on the back of motorcycles, but writes on Southern California for travel books and magazine articles, and has made radio guest appearances to discuss sightseeing in Southern California.

TABLE OF CONTENTS

Each tour in this guide is accompanied by a map and tour highlight section to help plan trips and for easy access to information while on the road. The enclosed maps are general layouts for each tour and are not intended to replace accurate and detailed road maps. Riding interests are defined by the terms S*labber, Meanderer*, and *Bender*. Each category is described below to help assist and match individual riding level with travels. In most tours, there are a variety of routes to choose from. You might also find other terms in this guide that you may or may not be familiar with. All riding terms and icons used are described below:

Slabber- A motorcyclist who prefers direct routes (super slab highways) for getting to a destination, like the Rock Store in the Santa Monica Mountains or Las Brisas at the shore in Laguna Beach. Slabbers select freeway routes over out of the way runs and shorter rides over *big dog runs*.

Meanderer- A motorcyclist who prefers the back roads over the freeway. A meanderer likes to go with the flow of touring, stopping to admire sights and to take in a good meal. Meanderers like challenging routes, and they clock the miles, but they are more interested in the trek itself than how many miles made it onto the odometer.

Bender- A motorcyclist who prefers to live in the saddle and clocks the miles, exploring every road and bend that crosses his or her path. A bender connects back roads and out of the way routes, avoiding freeways and straightaways and would eat riding, if at all possible. So much asphalt, so little time!

Crotch Rocket- A motorcyclist who prefers to ignore double yellows and speed postings, passing on curves at 60 mph, jittering the nerves of other riders, whizzing by like a wasp you can't bat at.

Big Dog Run- An all day ride of about 500 miles where you barely take time to gas up, eat, or soak in a view. Many motorcycle chapters organize big dog runs. Call your local Genuine Harley-Davidson dealer for more information on group touring.

A highlights section accompanies each tour and categorizes touring information into handbook form. These categories include road and weather conditions, restaurants, hotels, and attractions that are of interest to a rider who never wants to stray too far, or too long from the saddle. International road signs indicate food, gas, and lodging.

 indicates popular motorcycle spots.

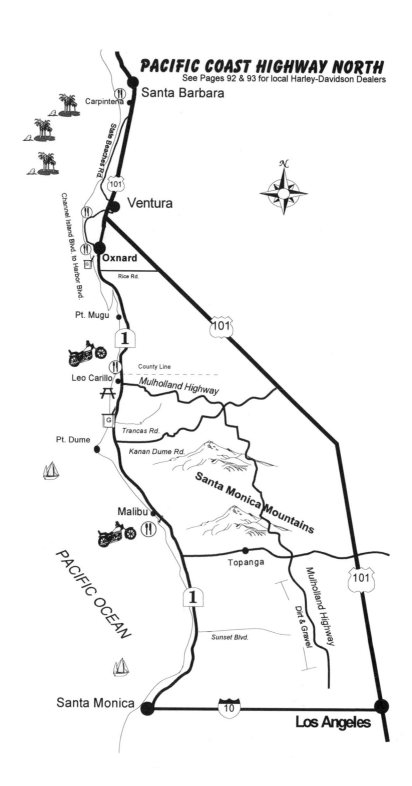

PACIFIC COAST HIGHWAY NORTH
See Pages 92 & 93 for local Harley-Davidson Dealers

Santa Barbara

Carpinteria

State Beaches Rd.

Channel Island Blvd. to Harbor Blvd.

101

Ventura

Oxnard

Rice Rd.

Pt. Mugu

1

Leo Carillo

County Line

Mulholland Highway

Trancas Rd.

Pt. Dume

Kanan Dume Rd.

Santa Monica Mountains

101

Malibu

Topanga

Mulholland Highway

Dirt & Gravel

101

PACIFIC OCEAN

1

Sunset Blvd.

Santa Monica

10

Los Angeles

PACIFIC COAST HIGHWAY NORTH

The trek across town on either **I-405** or **I-10,** west, to reach the **Pacific Coast Highway (PCH)** redefines *car*nivore and offers respectable argument for wearing a helmet. When the McClure tunnel finally appears and transforms city streets into sea and sand, a sigh of relief might seem in order, but keep those survival riding skills in the wings. Driving disorder is common in the free-spirited corridor, especially in the carnival-like beginning of the stretch during summer. If possible, arrive on the PCH before 10 a.m. on weekends. Travel against the crowds coming from and returning to the city during peak seasons and heat waves in February.

However, once you're through the McClure chute, no matter what time of day, riding the rim of the Pacific Coast is reason enough

to own a bike. Under clusters of palms, the California dream is in concentrated form. You can vicariously enjoy all activities from your first class seat—the scent of seafood platters salted by ocean breezes, colorful wind-surfers dipping in and out of swells, and even an occasional school of dolphins bodysurfing alongside sailboats and surfers.

On the other side of the highway, you'll see the weather worn cliffs supporting high dollar homes that have survived just about every natural disaster, and the interesting remains of those that have not.

In winter, the verdant hill-sides stretch for miles under billowy clouds. In spring, they blossom with wildflowers, pop-pies, and bougainvillea. In summer, they simply look more appealing than the gray blanket covering inland areas.

If you heed our advice and leave early, there are popular motorcycle stops from Santa Monica to County Line. You can get brunch, a bowl of chowder, or admire bikes with a drink.

Patrick's Road House is at the beginning of PCH, located at Channel Road behind the Chevron station. You might see a celebrity or two while having your bacon and eggs. The popular *Gladstone's* is also nearby at the base of Sunset Boulevard where you can order seafood omelets and cappuchinos on the outdoor patio if you beat the crowd. If you can't find parking out on the highway, you might be charged two bucks to park your bike on the lot.

The favorite spot of riders is *Malibu Inn*, located across from the pier at Surfrider beach. It has a casual atmosphere, good prices, and serves bender-sized portions. On Sunday mornings, guests arriving by iron horse receive preferential parking. How's that for a welcoming?

If you're holding out for lunch, farther up the coast is *Neptune's Net,* a casual seaside shanty with a sea of chrome parked outside its front porch. It's the hangout of choice for riders who aren't worried about dripping fresh cracked crab juice down their leathers, or for warming up with a bowl of homemade chowder on the outdoor patio.

Gas stops are frequent along the coast stretch until **Broad Beach Road** at Trancas Canyon. From there, the next gas opportunity is in the heart of Oxnard, about 25 miles north.

Traffic will gradually thin out as you ride up the coast and it's possible that just the pelicans will be your travel companions all the way to Oxnard. Beyond Trancas Canyon, you'll find a nice rhythm to the road as the black asphalt curls along the shoreline. At Pt. Mugu, there is a vantage point to enjoy the rugged beauty of this unpopulated coastal stretch.

The highway heads inland, and you'll follow herons into wetlands and then the crows into farmland. The strawberry fields will not last forever, and soon you'll find yourself on the cobblestone streets of old downtown Oxnard. You can avoid civilization for awhile by taking **Pleasant Valley Road**, left, to **Rice Road** exit off Hwy. 1 through another 10 miles of farmland which meets up with **Hwy. 101** in Camarillo.

If you like harbors or remaining by the coast, from Hwy. 1 take **Channel Islands Boulevard**, the main road into Port Hueneme and Ventura. At *Channel Islands Harbor,* a sleepy but growing little marina, you can find casual eating establishments. Continuing on Channel Islands Boulevard to **Harbor Boulevard** (the last street before the ocean), make a right and after a brief residential strip you can ride through undisturbed sand dunes and farmlands into Ventura. You'll come to *Ventura Harbor*, a modern seaside village with a variety of restaurants and trinket shops. *Andria's Seafood* is a picnic-bench style seafood eatery inside the harbor. For about the same menu price, you can get a view of the shore and docks from *Tuck's Point*, located in the mock lighthouse tower above the carousel. On weekends, the harbor has live music accompanying the sea breeze.

Proceeding on Harbor Boulevard, you'll link up with Hwy. 101 to continue up the coast toward Santa Barbara.

If you continue on Hwy. 1 through the cobblestone streets of old *Oxnard*, the short stretch is a first-hand experience on what it must be like to be Monty Montana in the Rose Parade. You'll receive plenty of appreciative nods and thumbs-ups from pedestrians as you rumble through town.

In this predominately Hispanic community you'll find fresh licuado and sandwich counters. Eating at one of the Mexican restaurants along the boulevard, like *Sal's Inn*, is as good as venturing across the border.

The last 6-mile stretch of Oxnard before linking up to Hwy. 101 will seem like a torture run as you endure the commercial district's chain store traffic. It is the quickest way back to the freeway, and once you enter, the gulls will appear again to escort you up the coast through Ventura and Santa Barbara.

At least three times a year, the big Harley-Davidson Swap Meet convenes at the Ventura County Fairground (also called Seaside Park.) The swaps are on a weekend generally in June, September, and December and you can confirm dates by calling (805) 648-3376. The Fairground is off the California Street exit.

By exiting a few miles past Ventura at **State Beaches** off-ramp, benders can ride parallel to the highway and close enough to the shoreline to play road tag with waves at high tide. Train enthusiasts can match their iron horse against the "big one" along this route as the track runs parallel to the road. You might be lucky to find yourself riding neck to neck with an Amtrak or freight train.

The beachfront road will last about 10 miles and then merge back on the freeway to continue up the coast. The next beach town is *Carpinteria*, one of the last traditional sleepy coastal communities. You can walk around town, soak in the sun with a libation on Chuy's restaurant patio, or eat a cheap but good steak at the landmark Palms on Linden Avenue in the center of town.

Continuing up the coast, 12 miles is Santa Barbara. Sightseeing is off the **Cabrillo Street** exit. *Stearn's Wharf* has a maritime museum and is the oldest walking pier in the state. It offers a whale's-eye view of the shoreline, and a variety of restaurants. *State Street* is located in this area, too.

The popular walking district is of old Spanish architecture where even McDonald's is housed under a tile roof. There are cafes, taverns, boutiques and bookshops for several blocks. Bakeries and coffee houses for a mid-afternoon pick-me-up can be found in every block. Casual pub-like places, such as *Joe's Cafe* and *Open Door*, have burgers and cheese sandwich steaks, as well as dinner.

To return home, follow your tire tracks along the coast or slab back south on Hwy. 101. Once back inside the Los Angeles basin, Hwy. 101 links up with most major freeways.

For more riding around the Santa Barbara area, see the San Marcos Pass/ Santa Maria Tour to continue up to Central California. See the Ojai Tour

for inland destinations and other connecting areas.

PACIFIC COAST HIGHWAY NORTH HIGHLIGHTS

Approximate Mileage: 205 miles round trip from Los Angeles.

Road Ratings:
PACIFIC COAST HIGHWAY/ MEANDERER; 2 - 4 lane highway, winding, scenic, can be congested from Santa Monica to Malibu.
HWY 101/ SLABBER; multi-lane, scenic in parts, congested in peak travel hours.
RICE RD./ SLABBER; 2-lane straightaway through farm fields.
CHANNEL ISLANDS BLVD./ SLABBER; 4-lane commercial and residential strip.
HARBOR BLVD./ SLABBER; 2 - 4 lane, scenic, residential and rural road.

Weather:
Usually breezy and 10 degrees cooler than inland temperatures.

Restaurants:
*Patrick's Road House,*Channel Rd. & PCH, Santa Monica.
Gladstones, Sunset Blvd. & PCH, Pacific Palisades.
Malibu Inn, 22969 PCH, across from Malibu Pier.
Neptune's Net, 42505 PCH at County Line.
*Sal's Inn,*1450 S. Oxnard Blvd., Oxnard.
Andria's Seafood, Ventura Harbor.
Stearn's Wharf & State Street, Santa Barbara.

Attractions:
Pt. Mugu
Seaport Village
Channel Islands State Park
Ventura Harbor
Ventura Old Town
State Street
Stearn's Wharf

Local Harley-Davidson Dealer:
VENTURA HARLEY-DAVIDSON, 1326 Del Norte Blvd., Camarillo, (805) 981-9904

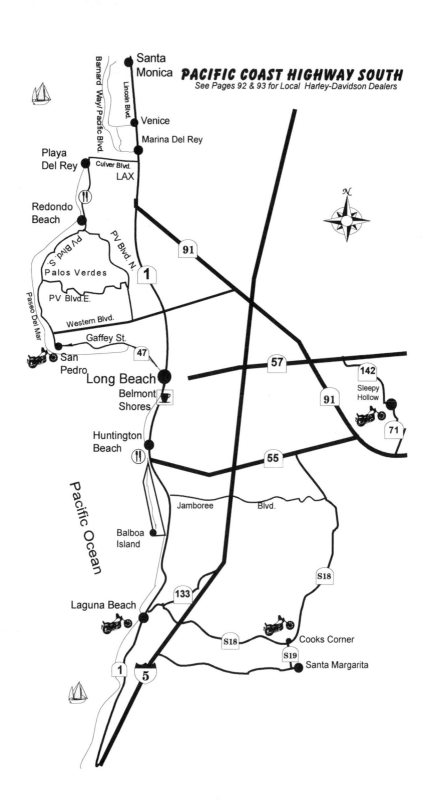

PACIFIC COAST HIGHWAY SOUTH
See Pages 92 & 93 for Local Harley-Davidson Dealers

PACIFIC COAST HIGHWAY SOUTH

If you're in the mood for being social and honoring the cruising credo, "live to ride, ride to eat," you'll love this Sunday scooter ride. There's nothing quite like a sunset spin in the refreshing breezes along the Pacific Coast Highway (PCH) especially when inland areas are summer infernos. It's an ideal route for beginners or just browsin' and carousin' as the coast has an abundance of scenic stops for stretching and sidewalk cafes for resting.

Starting at the McClure Tunnel that links up with PCH, north, the coast highway is shared with congested city living until Palos Verdes Peninsula. **Lincoln Boulevard** off **I-10** is Highway 1, the PCH through the Santa Monica Bay beaches. You can stay on Lincoln Boulevard to Sepulveda Boulevard through the LAX area, and Highway 1 will eventually hug the coast again in Orange County.

A more scenic route can be navigated through the bay beaches by taking the **4th Street** offramp from I-10, and turn left (south) to **Pico Boulevard** and dropping down to the Santa Monica's shores at **Barnard Way**. It will wrap along the coast to **Pacific Street**, where you continue south by turning right.

When you see men dressed like women, an army of ex-Vietnam Vets, and dogs adorned in bandanas, you've come to *Venice Beach*. The popular Boardwalk draws a motorcycle crowd at the base of **Windward Street**. You can easily spend the day here checking out the corral of iron horses, sampling international fare from food stands, and watching bizarre sidewalk shows while shaking Rottweilers off your new boots.

Past Windward Street, at the intersection of **Pacific and Washington Streets**, make a left and continue into the community of Marina Del Rey.

At any of the streets with Polynesian names, (Panawan, Mindanao, Bora Bora, etc.) you can make a right and take them through the Marina to admire the yachts or enjoy a brunch of eggs benedict.

Both Washington Boulevard and **Fiji Way** (inside the marina) will link you back up to **Lincoln Boulevard** to continue south. A short respite from city scenes will appear as you enter the Ballona Creek wetlands. At **Culver Boulevard**, turn right and follow the lush marsh into Playa Del Rey. A left turn at the coast is the gateway to all South Bay beaches.

The coastal route through Playa Del Rey is along sand dunes and a bluff overlooking the Pacific Ocean. LAX's flight path is enroute and it's possible a Boeing 747 to London will rise over the cliff like a steel Phoenix. Out to sea, huge tankers are usually filling up at the Chevron refinery.

After this stretch, Manhattan, Hermosa, and Redondo beaches are crammed pockets of populated living akin to a bean jar. In Manhattan you can play a road game—try to find a yard. Crowded but carefree, these coastal communities have a fine selection of sidewalk cafes where you can watch the beach scene come alive over coffee and huevos rancheros. After King's Harbor in Redondo Beach, the coastal environment changes radically into the ruggedness of Northern California.

However, the tile roofs and rambling Bougainvillea on Palos Verdes Peninsula retain the charm of Southern California.

Climbing the bluff into Palos Verdes (PV), you'll leave the ocean for a brief jaunt along Palos Verdes Drive South. It's easy to get around the incredibly scenic and peaceful peninsula as the streets form a loop and are simply named Palos Verdes Drive South, North, East, and West.

PV Boulevard North is a 4-lane road that meanders through an area of eucalyptus woods with bridal paths and lots of shade. At the the intersection of **PV Drive East**, make a right and wind up and over a crest, then down to the sea with views of the skyline. There's a turn-out, about 1/2-mile from the intersection, where you can absorb an 180-degree view, a perfect place to enjoy a packed snack. Beware though, while the butterflies flitter before your eyes, a rattlesnake might be slithering at your feet. You'll be glad you wore hightops.

Continuing down to the coast a section of the road with 15-mph turns does attract an occasional crotch rocket to jerk you from any Zen state back into the L.A. energy belt. Also in the area is light residential traffic that usually maintains a good clip on the curves.

PV Drive South offers the best views of contorted Portuguese Bend and the Los Angeles metropolis. A right will lead back toward the South Bay and all the peninsula's points of interest. The first one is quickly realized as you ignore the first dip sign and become airborne. You're on Portuguese Bend.

This contorted, continually shifting land mass requires ongoing street work through a short stretch where road cautions should be taken literally. For once you can be thankful your home is inland where a driveway does not lead to the bedroom window.

After Portuguese Bend, within a mile and on the bluff is the *Wayfarer's Church*, designed by Frank Lloyd Wright. Its glass architecture is intended to reflect upon and inspire those at sea. The church and lovely gardens are always busy with weddings but are also open to the public.

Next to highlight the landscape is the weathered Marineland landmark, and then *Pt. Vincente lighthouse*. A park runs along the cliffs with an awesome coastline view comparable to any in Oregon. From this vantage point, you're bound to see whales in winter. There's no better place to run to after a bad day at work.

A left turn from PV Drive East onto PV Drive South will lead to San Pedro. At Western Boulevard, make a right to **Paseo Del Mar** where you continue to hug the coast. Near White's Point is an expansive tide pool worth bringing a pair of sneakers to explore in low tide. Pt. Fermin Lighthouse is at the opening of the harbor where you can watch the freighters hit the sea. On Paseo Del Mar is *Walker's Cafe*, a popular motorcycle hangout where you can grab a bite or a drink and share stories from Portuguese Bend.

Paseo Del Mar will dead-end onto **Gaffey Street.** Take a left and follow the signs to drop down to **Harbor Boulevard** to ride along the harbor. You'll pass *Ports 'O Call*, the tourist seaside village where you can grab a Corona out of an ice chest while a fresh piece of fish is cooked to order on outdoor barbeques. Dine on a festive, outdoor patio and watch the big ships roll in.

Vincent Thomas Bridge, Hwy. 47, has a connector ramp from Harbor Boulevard and is toll free from the northern end. The lengthy, steel-laced path plops you on Terminal Island which houses prisons and defunct shipyards. Continue on to Long Beach and the stately Queen Mary which you can visit by following the signs.

The bridge turns into **Ocean Street** in the heart of Long Beach. This was Los Angeles' first seaside playland until a fire wiped out the fancy hotels and ballrooms. *Shoreline Village* is now Long Beach's most popular tourist spot with its wharf and restaurants and trinket shops. *Shoreline Park* offers a scenic stretch stop with a view of the Queen Mary across the waterway.

Long Beach might be gaining back a reputation for amusements, but its neighbor to the south, *Belmont Shores,* is the more popular strip for cruising the chrome. Established sidewalk cafes and a traditional beach scene is just what bikers want. Ocean Avenue will become **2nd Street**, crossing over canals to enter the quaint and quiet community of Naples.

Past Naples you'll ride along the area's older marinas and discover where the San Gabriel River finally meets the sea. Over a bridge PCH will appear, and you'll go through a lagoon to enter Orange County and Seal Beach. To drop down

to Seal Beach's municipal pier and boardwalk, take **Main Street**. In this tucked away beach town, you might actually find a parking spot.

PCH will return to a commercial strip briefly, but converts back into a coastal strip of fun-in-the-sun through Orange County. There's something to see and eat in every beach town from Sunset Beach to San Clemente.

Sunset Beach has a good diner right on the highway and still possess an old fashioned beach charm. Near Warner Boulevard, there is a saltwater lagoon with birdwatching footpaths to stroll if you're in need of burning off a meal to make room for another.

In Huntington Beach, state beaches allow campfires, and at sunset their flames glitter in the twilight glow while scenting the salt air. Put a swim suit under the saddle and escape here during the dog days of summer.

Along PCH, it will seem that everyone loves a motorcycle parade, but in Huntington Beach the police just love to ticket them. Loud pipes put a popular Thai restaurant with its motorcycling crowd out of business. The moral to the story is don't get on the throttle within city limits.

If you can stay out of

trouble, Huntington Beach does have a festive atmosphere. A renovated Main Street runs into the coast by the pier with outdoor cafes and original '60s surf shops.

Next-in-line beach communities are Newport Beach and Balboa Island. Balboa Boulevard will take you out to a seaside original pier and amusement arcade with games and Balboa ice cream bars. Unless you ferry over to Balboa Island, you must backtrack to get on PCH toward Laguna Beach.

In Newport Beach you can ride east on **Jamboree Boulevard** to a Hard Rock Cafe in Fashion Island. You can continue up Jamboree to S18 and Cook's Corner, the popular motorcycle hangout.

The stretch between Newport and Laguna Beach is a welcome, non-commercial area where you can break free if there is light traffic.The coast changes from recreational flat lands to a more rugged environment with curves on cliffs rising from the sea.

Las Brisas restaurant in Laguna is a popular destination for Harley riders where one can chat and chew overlooking the emerald ocean. As motorcycle parking was becoming anarchistic, there is now a strict,

one-bike-per-meter rule if there is no space in the parking lot.

Laguna is a picturesque coastal enclave with small shops, galleries, and cafes along its rocky shore. Don't forget to wave at the statue of the famous "Laguna Greeter" who was a community mascot during the '60s and '70s. Occasionally, someone tries to take over, but no one can duplicate his Rip Van Winkle style.

To visit venerable Cook's Corner, take **Hwy. 133** from Laguna to **S18, (El Toro Road** then **Santiago Road,)** and continue inland. Hwy. 133 is a pretty ride through a eucalyptus forest trying to recover from the '93 fires. It's also the home of the famous Laguna Beach Arts Festival. S18 is a right fork off the highway.

S18 first requires a journey across a suburban sea. After I-5 and a brief 6-lane, commercial stretch, S18 transforms into a 4-lane country road. At the junction with **S19 (Live Oak Canyon Road)** there will be a herd of motorcycles. You've arrived.

Cook's Corner is such a popular hangout, many bikers make a beeline here to kill an afternoon. The spacious establishment is a cafe, bar, and pool hall with outdoor seating for fresh air types. Every night there is some form of live entertainment.

If you're interested in a short scenic putt or wish to loop back to PCH or I-5, venture on S19. It's a wooded area, nice enough to house campgrounds. However, its serenity is short lived. You'll come to the town of Santa Margarita, a chameleonic maze of condo living and a labryrinth to leave! See if you can find a way out other than Hwy. 241, a toll road. However, by paying the fee, you'll get back to S18. If you can find Antonia Parkway, you can take it to Oso Parkway, west, and that will intersect with I-5 to Hwy. 133 to the PCH.

Continuing on S18, or Santiago Road, is also a pleasant run with sweeping curves that open up into racey stretches— good practice pavement for novices while enjoying pastures, creeks, and canyon crests with views. Many of the canyons have inviting roads that will lure you down their crevices, but they all dead end and you'll have to back track out. Silverado Canyon is one of the more popular treks into the belly of the Cleveland National Forest. S18 will link up with Jamboree Road, I-5, and I-55 via Chapman and Katella Avenues.

It's hip to hop from Cook's Corner to *Lavita's*, the other popular Orange County hangout in the back country. There is no easy scenic road connecting the two places. You can take Fwy. 57 to **Lambert Avenue** and then make a left onto **Carbon Canyon**, or take **Fwy. 91** to **Hwy. 71** and make a left onto Carbon Canyon. (This way is under construction to become an expressway.) Lavita's, on Carbon Canyon, is in Sleepy Hollow, but don't let the name fool you. Live music fills the hills on weekends and the place is always buzzing with activity and fun. A hot spring is nearby.

Carbon Canyon is a pretty putt with a regional park and lake. The road is full of nice riding curves, but you generally can't take advantage of them due to the high volume of traffic. It's usually just a means to an end... at Lavita's.

Other tours in the area are PCH North from the Santa Monica Bay area and Ortega Highway from Orange County. You can also easily link up with South San Diego for a weekend of riding.

PACIFIC COAST HIGHWAY SOUTH HIGHLIGHTS

Approximate Mileage: 180 miles round trip from Los Angeles

Road Ratings:
PACIFIC COAST HIGHWAY/ MEANDERER; 4-lane, commercial, traffic,
    scenic.
PACIFIC, OCEAN AVENUES/ MEANDERER; 4-lane, commercial, traffic,
    scenic.
PALOS VERDES DRIVES, N, S, E, W/ MEANDERER; curves, hills, scenic.
HWY. 133/ MEANDERER; 4-lane, curves, scenic.
S18 & S19/ MEANDERER; curves, scenic, good practice, commercial.
CARBON CANYON / MEANDERER; curves, heavy traffic, scenic.

Weather:
Generally cooler than inland areas, spring through fall. Afternoon
breezes are common.

Restaurants:
Walker's Cafe, 700 Paseo Del Mar, San Pedro. (310) 833-3623
Las Brisas, 361Cliff Drive, Laguna Beach. (714) 497-5434.
Lavita's, 6105 Carbon Canyon Road, Brea. (714) 996-0720

Attractions:

Venice Beach Boardwalk	Ports 'O Call
Pt. Vincente Lighthouse	Wayfarer's Chapel
Belmont Shores	Shoreline Village

Local Harley-Davidson Dealers:
BARTELS' HARLEY-DAVIDSON, 4141 Lincoln Blvd., Marina Del Rey,
    (310) 823-1112
CALIFORNIA HARLEY-DAVIDSON, 1517 Pacific Coast Highway, Harbor
    City, (310) 539-3366
HARLEY-DAVIDSON OF WESTMINSTER, 13031 Goldenwest St. Westminster,
    (714) 893-6274
LOS ANGELES HARLEY-DAVIDSON, 13300 Paramount Blvd., South Gate
    (562) 408-6088
ORANGE COUNTY HARLEY-DAVIDSON, 8677 Research Dr., Irvine,
    (949) 727-4464
POMONA VALLEY HARLEY-DAVIDSON, 8710 Central Ave., Montclair,
    (909) 981-9500, (near Lavita's)

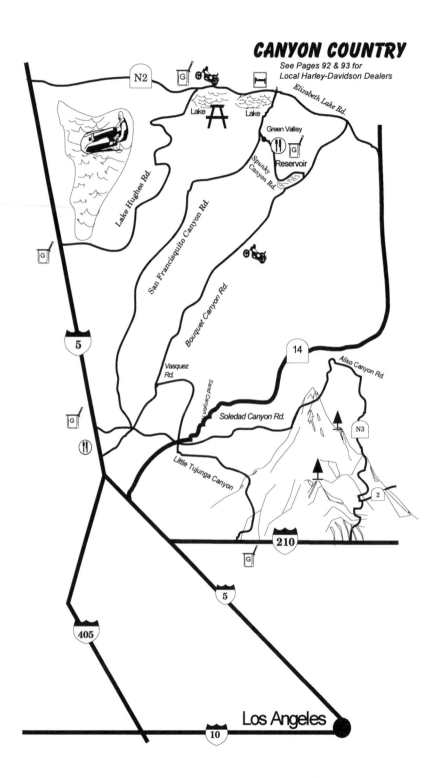

CANYON COUNTRY

See Pages 92 & 93 for
Local Harley-Davidson Dealers

N2

Elizabeth Lake Rd.

Lake

Lake

Green Valley

Reservoir

Spunky Canyon Rd.

Lake Hughes Rd.

San Francisquito Canyon Rd.

Bouquet Canyon Rd.

Vasquez Rd.

14

Aliso Canyon Rd.

Sand Canyon Rd.

Soledad Canyon Rd.

N3

5

Little Tujunga Canyon

2

210

5

405

Los Angeles

10

CANYON COUNTRY / ANGELES FOREST

Thrill rides aren't confined to Magic Mountain in Canyon Country. Outside L.A.'s back door, bikers can find some of the best riding terrain at all skill levels. Add panoramic views, river chasing, moonscape settings, and a diner burger for the perfect day, equal to that of any kid sacrificing his lunch over Viper.

Start your ride by getting to Lake View Terrace, located off the **Osborne Boulevard** exit from **I-210**. If you come from the west, make a right onto **Foothill Boulevard** and then a quick left onto Osborne. It will turn into **Little Tujunga Road**, an 18-mile jog that follows a stream through grassy chaparral.

In addition to slide watches, look for an occasional stray peacock. The area teems with birds on land as well as in the fresh, sage-scent air. If you look off in the distance and see a caged lion or alligator, that's part of the *Wildlife Way Station*, a home for orphaned exotic pets. You can stop and visit the menagerie on the 1st and 3rd Sunday of each month by calling (818) 899-5201.

Little Tujunga Road becomes twisty about 8 miles into the ride. Novice riders might find the terrain more challenging than enjoyable. Think of it as a practice session for mastering your machine. (You can also super slab your way into Santa Clarita by taking 1-5 to **Hwy. 14** and exit at **Sand Canyon Road**.)

Little Tujunga Road is a gradual climb to a crest where, besides excellent road conditions, you'll find an everlasting view at the top. On a clear day you'll see Frazier Park to the northeast and the peaks of the Los Padres National Forest range to the north.

Descending through a canopy of trees to lower elevations, you can warm up while admiring a pocket of grand estates for modern Will Rogers types. Notice how many of the barns for resident's pets are nicer than homes in the basin. When the road forks, bear right onto **Sand Canyon Road**. Before continuing, you might want to pull up the bandana to avoid a facial scrub. Often, there's a windy blast for several miles until you cross the highway and find shelter in the hills along Vasquez Road.

Gas is available at the highway junction. Continue on Sand Canyon to **Sierra Highway**, make a right, and look immediately for **Vasquez Canyon Road** on the left.

You can see *Vasquez Rocks,* a cluster of smooth boulders (where they filmed the Flinstones,) by continuing on Sierra Highway to Agua Dulce Road, turning right and following the signs. The boulders honor the bandit Tiburcio Vasquez, train robber and cattle thief, who used them as a hide out.

Back to Vasquez Road, the route is generally protected from wind and is a nice ride through ranch country, free of traffic and stops and loaded with mountain views. When Vasquez Road intersects with **Bouquet Canyon Road**, turn right and continue on into the gorge. You'll travel along a creek that keeps the canyon refreshing and lush. In winter, the string of stark and stocky deciduous trees have a haunting appearance, but in spring, they rejuvenate the countryside with a blossoming canopy of fresh leaves. Tucked off the road are funky cabins that suggest mighty interesting people live in them.

About 7 miles into the canyon is *Big Oak Lodge*, a biker spot with restaurant, bar, and outside barbeque for quick sandwiches. Motorcycle clubs and professional groups like to pack the place. It's reliably open seven days a week. On weekend evenings you can take a twilight run up for dinner and live music.

Continuing on Bouquet Canyon, set the throttle for comfortable cruising and enjoy the curves and scenery. The road will narrow, and sand or water pockets in shady areas can creep up. As the road ascends, Bouquet Canyon Reservoir will be a trail marker for **Spunky Canyon Road** where you'll turn left.

Spunky Canyon Road runs along the reservoir and will continue to ascend onto a benderish, roller coaster run with sandy grades. Novices should take their time. As the elevation rises, the temperature will drop, sometimes up to a 20-degree temperature change from the L.A. basin. Bring clothes to add an extra layer so you can enjoy the higher elevations without shivering.

Green Valley is a small (and

we mean small) town along the way. It does have two essentials for survival, a liquor store and the *Green Valley Cafe,* a community center with bar and pool table. You'll notice the strong community relations—everyone is on a personal, first name basis.

After you warm up with a tea or cool down with a soda continue northwest on Spunky Canyon until **San Francisquito Canyon Road** (be glad it's not your address). You can either turn right to continue on for more spectacular scenery, or take a left if you're ready to join up with I-5.

Benders who make the right will continue onto **Lake Elizabeth Road, N2.** Make a left and travel past two lakes to the *Rock Inn,* an old stage stop and lodge now buzzing with bikers. If you over eat, over drink, or get over tired, spend the night in one of the guest rooms upstairs.

After Lake Hughes, look for **Lake Hughes Road** from Elizabeth Lake Road and make a left. Even though the lake looks like a pond compared to the other bodies of water in the area, the road is subject to floods and can remain wet with sandy patches even in droughts. The area offers public recreation for picnics and camping, and down the road you'll even find a covered wagon

ring for group parties.

Lake Hughes Road gets a gold star for both riding fun and scenery, lots of curves hugging the hillside, and runs from shaded glens to majestic vista points. Brick red rock formations with contrasting verdant patches will enhance an already spectacular ride.

Curves relinquish the road into a stretch of grade that runs above Castaic Lake, a scenic vantage point to watch activities on the lake without the crowds. (There's a good chance you'll hit wind again in the area.)

Continuing on Lake Hughes Road to I-5, you can gas up and then hop on the freeway, south to return to Los Angeles. Diehard benders will exit at **Hwy. 126,** east, (Magic Mountain Parkway) to wind the back roads home.

Stay on Hwy. 126 to **Valencia Boulevard** where you'll make a left. It will turn into **Soledad Canyon Road.** For a stretch on Soledad you'll be in a commercial area, a 6-lane road which will revert from mega malls back to mom and pop businesses. After the road parallels the freeway for a stretch, it will cut under Hwy. 14 and open up again to a winding, 2-lane country road with scattered residences.

The landscape will transform into more of a "Marscape" as you enter into a barren, reddish, rocky area, similar to Vasquez Rocks. You'll chase a river through the countryside.

Soledad Canyon will lead to the horse community of Acton. At **Aliso Canyon Road**, make a right to enjoy a newly paved trail with dips and turns to spark a second road wind. When you get to **N3** make another right and head for the hills. At the junction with **Angeles Highway, Hwy. 2,** make one last right. The ride through the mountainous Angeles Forest is a delightful freedom finale before ending up on the I-210 off Hwy. 2. The freeway will feel mighty strange after 290 miles of pure joy riding.

If the thought of a 290-mile, 1-day jaunt has you rubbing your rear, you can re-route the journey by taking any of the major canyon roads (Sand, Bouquet, Soledad, etc.) back to Hwy. 14 or I-5 and slab home.

There are other roads to explore in Canyon Country. **Old Ridge Road** near Lake Hughes Road by Castaic Lake is one of the oldest, scenic back roads in the area, always recommended in motoring travel guides. It is paved for about 10 miles to Templin Highway and then turns to dirt.

Taking N2 (Elizabeth Lake Road) to **Willow Springs Road** to **Lancaster Road**, left, will lead to the *Antelope Valley Poppy Reserve* in Lancaster. This is a rewarding side trip from March through May to see the orange poppy and purple lupine carpet along the hills. Down the street from the Poppy Reserve at 557 W. Lancaster Blvd. is the *Western Hotel*, an 1880 landmark, perfectly preserved and has free daily tours of its rooms.

N2 runs along the San Andreas Fault, and thrill seekers or geology buffs can examine the active fault's nooks and crannies from Hungry Valley to Palmdale. You can hop on the Angeles Highway near Palmdale and return to the Los Angeles area via the mountains as previously described. Other tours in the area are Angeles Crest Highway, Lake Isabella, and Ojai Tours.

CANYON COUNTRY HIGHLIGHTS

Approximate Mileage: 290 miles round trip from Los Angeles

Road Ratings:

LITTLE TUJUNGA RD./ MEANDERER; scenic, uncrowded, curves.
SAND CYN. RD./ VASQUEZ CYN. RD. MEANDERER; scenic, rolling.
BOUQUET CYN. RD./ MEANDERER; scenic, water/ sand pockets, curves.
SAN FRANCISQUITO CYN. RD./ MEANDERER; riding variety, scenic.
ELIZABETH LAKE (N2)/ MEANDERER; scenic, intersects other routes.
SPUNKY CYN. RD./ BENDER; scenic climb, sand, dips.
LAKE HUGHES RD./ MEANDERER; water pockets, well-paved,
    intersects other routes.
SOLEDAD CYN. RD./ MEANDERER & SLABBER; multi- to 2- lane road,
    commercial and scenic country portions.
N3 (ANGELES FOREST)/ MEANDERER; mountainous, scenic, landslides.
OLD RIDGE RD./ MEANDERER; 2-lane, Scenic historic route, views,
    older pavement, gravel portions.

Weather:
Extremes in elevation create temperature changes by 10 to 20
degrees. Layered clothing suggested.

Restaurants:
BigOak Lodge, 3310 Bouquet Cyn. Rd., Saugus. (661) 296-5656
Tony's Hideaway Cafe, 15488 Spunky Cyn. Rd., Grass Vly. (661) 270-9118
Rock Inn, 17539 Lake Elizabeth Rd., Saugus. (661) 724-1855

Attractions:
Vasquez Rocks
Lake Elizabeth and Hughes
Antelope Valley Poppy Reserve, Lancaster Road at 110th St. West,
    Lancaster. (661) 942-0662 or 724-1180
Western Hotel, 557 W. Lancaster Blvd., Lancaster. (661) 723-6250

Local Harley-Davidson Dealers:
HARLEY-DAVIDSON OF LANCASTER, 45313 23rd St., Lancaster,
    (661) 948-5959

SANTA PAULA/ OJAI/ LOCKWOOD VALLEY

See Page 92 & 93 for Local Harley-Davidson Dealers

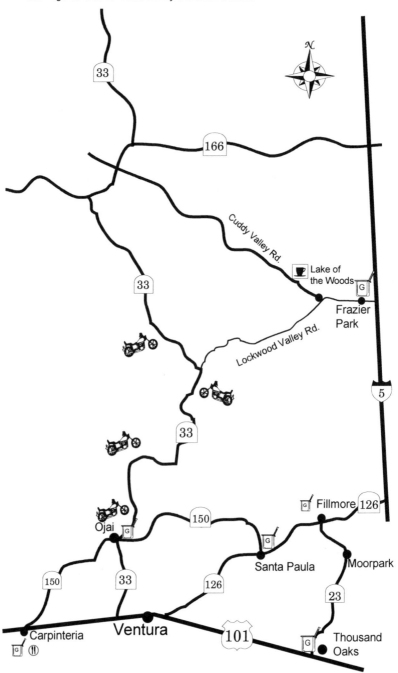

Discovering the backroads of Ventura County, your throttle thumbs will have you returning again and again. On this 280-mile round trip ride, you'll feel like an escaped thoroughbred traveling through Arizona, Utah, and Colorado.

There is both a super slab and a bender route to enjoy this one day jaunt. The more scenic, round-the-bend way begins on **Hwy. 101**, north, through San Fernando Valley to **Hwy. 23**, north, to Moorpark. Take **Los Angeles Avenue** exit, west, that links up to Hwy. 23 again after the community of Moorpark. Follow the signs to Hwy. 23 through the 25-mph business zone. The road breaks into a fun curve run which you'll know is coming up by the smell of a chicken ranch.

The terrain turns mountainous through Oak Ridge, and the road enters into a canyon that overlooks the Santa Clara River. You'll come to Fillmore after the scenic pocket where you can obtain food and gas. The next town 9 miles to the west is *Santa Paula*, located at the junction of **Hwy. 126** and **Hwy. 150**. This quaint and quiet walking community is a pleasant place to stretch and remove the road hum from your ears.

For petroleum buffs, there is a *Union Oil Museum* with interesting exhibits on local crude history. It's usually open Thursdays through Sundays.

Also a central packing and transportation area for citrus and avocado farming, Santa Paula has a historic train station. The depot is often used for location filming for movies and television. Special events are sometimes scheduled. (See Highlights Section for more information.)

Continuing on **Hwy. 150**, north, the curvy road enters into a wooded area following the Santa Paula Creek. It's possible that you'll end up sharing the narrow route with a farm truck through the canyon. There is no passing in this section, but don't get frustrated over the slow travel. You'll get plenty of opportunity to break loose up ahead.

Out of the canyon, the terrain will open up into an agricultural valley, laced with white picket fences and clusters of flowers. It will descend into Ojai Valley. A 1/2-mile portion of the ride is full of twists that might intimidate novice riders. After that, the only twists and contortions into Ojai will be the trunks and branches of the old oak trees.

Acres of fragrant fruit trees are also enroute and many of the farms advertise fresh produce. In some orchards you can even pick your own if you don't mind a little dirt on your boots and can figure out how to get the pickings home.

The town of Ojai lies ahead and primarily appeals to the New Age culture, art collectors, and used book scavengers. The latter head to *Bart's Books*, located at the corner of Canada and Matilija Streets. An entire house and its courtyard is dedicated to the shelving of 100,000 used books, from glass-cased collectibles to trashy paperback novels.

Rather than mill around Ojai, most scooterists continue through town and make a right onto **Hwy. 33** (you have to really watch for the turnoff) and ride 2 miles to the *Deer Lodge*, a popular stop for food and drink.

From the lodge you can either return to Hwy. 150 and continue west into Carpinteria or continue on Hwy. 33, north, toward Pine Mountain Summit, Lockwood Valley and Frazier Park. Either route you choose, take the other one the next time.

By taking Hwy. 150, west, to Lake Casitas you'll meander through a romantic California landscape of beautiful homes and ranches set to a backdrop of citrus and avocado groves. The hilly terrain will lead to the sandy shores of Carpinteria where you can link up with the coast highway. (See Pacific Coast Highway North Tour.)

Continuing on Hwy. 33, is also a popular ride, particularly with crotch rockets. However, it will lead to Lockwood Valley Road, usually a traffic free trail, and one of the most breathtaking rides in Southern California.

Leaving Deer Lodge, Hwy. 33 will become surrounded with steep, jagged cliffs and rock climbers all over them. Down below them, fishermen and swimmers enjoy Matilija Creek. A retreat, Wheeler Springs, is just a turn off the highway if you're in the mood for a pricey but relaxing hot mineral bath.

Most riders prefer to stay dusty and revved up to climb

out of the gorge and along the mountain tops. The 2-lane road provides excellent riding conditions. About 20-miles from Ojai you'll find another biker spot, *Wolf Inn,* a one-of-a-kind establishment with live-stock farm, shooting range and hanging dollar bill collection. Nearby the lodge, huge oak trees will seem bonsai"ed" against the biggest boulders this side of Jupiter's moons.

After shooting the breeze and admiring other Big Twins, saddle up for more scenic wonders ahead. Once past Pine Mountain Summit there is more climbing into the timberline and then back down via curving and sandy conditions for 10 miles into Lockwood Valley. This bad case of road dandruff, created by cliff erosion, can be just as annoying as the occasional crotch rocket, and both should be watched out for in the area.

Reaching the edge of Lockwood Valley, you'll ride through pine trees that look as if a florist arranged them in the rich, red rock formations. In the distance a breathtaking view is composed of endless mountain ridges and an expansive valley floor.

At the junction of **Lockwood Valley Road** and Hwy. 33 you can either continue on the highway to Santa Maria and Bakersfield or onto Lockwood

Valley Road toward Frazier Park.

Continuing on Hwy. 33 leads to the *Halfway Station and* the *Song Dog Ranch.* Bringing along only a bedroll and toothbrush, you can stay comfortably at the ranch which provides tents and meals. Groups and clubs are welcome, too.

Continuing on Lockwood Valley Road, you'll pass a water crossing about 2 miles into the stretch. About 4 miles from the junction, look for a wood-stained sign directing you 1-1/2 miles down a gravelly side road to *Camp Scheideck Lodge.* Another original, overnight establishment, the century old homestead is a creekside campground and lodge.

The lodge's burgers are very good, but ask the cook to go easy on the salt if you're ordering fries. You can take your food out to the deck or eat inside while watching pool sharks at work. House rules warn that jumping the cue ball mandates a slow song on the jukebox.

Besides the scenic splendor it provides, Lockwood Valley Road itself is a treat. Revel on the deep dips over the straight-away; just make sure there's no deep pool of water in those troughs!

After the roller coaster stretch, the road will ascend into

the timberline again. By making a right turn onto **Frazier Mountain Road,** you'll reach the community of Frazier Park and then 1-5. Slabbing south on 1-5 will take you back toward Los Angeles.

1-5 is the alternative, super slab route into Ventura County mentioned at the beginning of the chapter. It also links up with Hwy. 126, west. Now a 4-lane route, Hwy. 126 is safe yet scenic—a fun slabber's ride. There is usually heavy RV travel to all the fresh water lakes in the area. Fillmore and Santa Paula, as well as the opportunity to link up with Hwy. 150 and Hwy. 33 are all reachable coming from this way.

If you want to continue on back trails from Lockwood Valley, grab a cup of coffee and pastry at the deli in Lake of the Woods and instead of turning onto Frazier Mountain Road, continue on **Cuddy Valley Road** for more supremo trails.

Cuddy Valley Road will become **Mil Potrero** where you'll want to stay to the right. About 8-miles from the transition is the small community of Pine Mountain where you'll find gas, good food and shops to look in if you want to stretch.

Continuing on Mil Potrero from Pine Mountain there will be a crossing for **Cerro**

Noroeste Road. Take it right and open up the throttle into a great little run of sweeping curves (and sometimes deer) that will link up again with Hwy. 33 or Hwy. 166. The road is a real treat with 5000-foot elevations and few travelers. Try it in spring when there's lush green hills and wildflowers.

Before adventuring toward Cerro Noroeste Road from Pine Mountain, it's wise to check conditions at the local gas station or call ahead to the Los Padres National Forest. The road is sometimes closed due to rain or repair.

(See Kern River, Santa Maria and Canyon Country Tours.)

SANTA PAULA/ OJAI/ LOCKWOOD VALLEY HIGHLIGHTS

Approximate Mileage: 280 miles round trip from Los Angeles

Road Ratings:
HWY 101/ SLABBER; multi-lane straightaway with hills.
HWY. 23/ MEANDERER; multi-lane straightaway to twisting rural route.
HWY. 126/ MEANDERER; 2-lane, scenic, curves, hills.
HWY. 150/ BENDER; 2-lane, scenic, curves, hills.
HWY. 33/ BENDER; 2-lane, mountainous, sandy patches.
LOCKWOOD VALLEY ROAD/ MEANDERER; 2-lane, dips, curves, scenic.

Weather:
Dress in layers year round. Most pleasant riding is generally from May to October. In winter, there can be snow on the ground at higher elevations, and I-5 can close near Frazier Park.

Restaurants:
Deer Lodge, 2261 Maricopa Hwy. (805) 646-4256
Wolf Inn, 30 mi. NE of Ojai on Hwy. 33,
        Open Thurs. - Sun.
Camp Scheideck Lodge, Lockwood Valley Rd., Maricopa,
        Open May - Sept.
Halfway Station, Hwy. 33, past Lockwood Valley junction.
Lake of the Woods Deli, Lake of the Woods

Accommodations:
Song Dog Ranch, camping (805) 766-2454
Camp Scheideck, camping (805) 649-9738
Lake Casitas, camping (805) 654-3951

Attractions:
Union Oil Museum, 1001 E. Main St., Santa Paula.
Santa Paula Train Station (805) 933-1277

Local Harley-Davidson Dealer:
BARGER HARLEY-DAVIDSON, 22107 Sherman Way, Canoga Park,
        (818) 999-3355
VENTURA HARLEY-DAVIDSON, 1326 Del Norte Blvd., Camarillo,
        (805) 981-9904

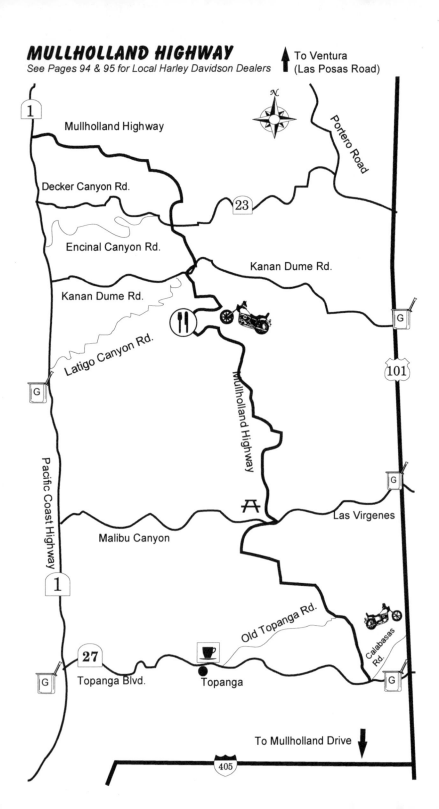

MULLHOLLAND HIGHWAY
See Pages 94 & 95 for Local Harley Davidson Dealers

To Ventura
(Las Posas Road)

N

Mullholland Highway

Portero Road

Decker Canyon Rd.

23

Encinal Canyon Rd.

Kanan Dume Rd.

Kanan Dume Rd.

G

Latigo Canyon Rd.

101

G

G

Mullholland Highway

1

G

Las Virgenes

Malibu Canyon

Pacific Coast Highway

1

Old Topanga Rd.

Calabasas Rd.

27

G

Topanga Blvd.

Topanga

G

To Mullholland Drive

405

MULLHOLLAND HIGHWAY

The Mullholland run is to motorcycling what Wimbledon is to tennis and Pebble Beach is to golf. The rite of passage into the sport is finding a parking spot at the Rock Store.

Several canyon routes intersect with Mullholland Highway, which runs along the crest of the Santa Monica Mountains. These runs provide all levels of ideal riding through a variety of canyons.

Mullholland Highway and Drive, named after the Irishman who engineered the famous aqueduct expressway from far away Owens Valley to Los Angeles, runs from the Hollywood Hills to the surf by Ventura County line. However, through Topanga State Park the road turns from pavement to dirt and gravel for seven miles and tends to divide Mullholland into two sections. North of Topanga Canyon is the more popular portion and site of the Rock Store.

Mullholland Highway is reachable off the Pacific Coast Highway through several canyons or Hwy. 101, with the PCH being the preferred route. Mullholland is an easy putt on a 2-lane, scenic road with nice sweeping curves and a few challenging spots for interest.

Ranches and designer homes are roadside attractions until Malibu. The road then dissects Malibu State Park with fun climbs and curves along the roaming chaparral.

Approaching Westlake Village, if the hills come alive with the theme from *Mash* that's because the '70s television show was filmed nearby. You're zooming in on the show's opening aerial shot as you ride through these hills.

So many crotch rockets like to buzz through the stretch between Malibu and Latigo Canyons, you might guess that this is near the *Rock Store*.

When you come around a bend and are blinded by chrome reflection, you've arrived at the Rock Store. There is protocol to follow at this venerable hangout. Harley-Davidson bike owners park their iron horses on the ocean side of the dirt lot and the imports huddle on the Valley side. The lookey-loos in cars who want to see a two-wheeling celebrity like Jay Leno park on the street.

Once parking is achieved, patrons spend their time checking out bikes, sharing road tales, eating, drinking, and signing the petitions of motorcycle advocates. On the shady patio, sheltered by a huge oak tree, the menu is barbequed tri-tip and beer. Inside the cabin-like landmark there is a restaurant with more beer and a store which stocks motorcycling souvenirs.

Continuing toward the ocean on Mullholland, the road will gnarl into a 3-mile section of tight twists, then relax again into less critical maneuvering. There are several canyon routes off Mullholland that all lead to the coast. (See individual descriptions of roads.) Staying on Mullholland is a pretty ride to the coast, with a few more critical pockets and a final run through the lush and cool Leo Carrillo State Park before ending at the Pacific Coast Highway.

Each canyon run in the area has its own riding personality and degree of difficulty. They are briefly described below.

Topanga Canyon Boulevard (Hwy. 27) - This is one of the more travelled routes by car as well as motorcycle. The scenic, 2-lane highway travels alongside Topanga State Park.

You can get a snack or coffee in the hippie-like village of Topanga with its funky community center and natural food stores. Beyond Topanga center there are a few more retail pockets with cafes and bars.

The most critical area on this stretch is the first set of climbing twists as you enter the canyon. All too frequently, an impatient motorcyclist will try to pass a 1968 sedan with bad rings, and won't make the narrow squeeze between it and on-coming traffic. It's not worth the risk as the road will open up ahead.

Old Topanga Road- Located off Hwy. 27 near Topanga town center, Old Topanga Road is not only more scenic, but is an isolated alternative for reaching Mullholland Highway. The narrow road is a more intimate ride with the surroundings and allows for examining the primal cliffs and the big boulders that rest precariously upon them. This route is also cooler in the summer as it is closer to the coast. The twists in the road require a bit more skill than those on Hwy. 27, but with the freedom from traffic, you can take your time. Once you get to Mullholland Highway, take a left to continue on to the Rock Store.

Malibu Canyon- (*Las Virgenes Road from Hwy. 101.*) This is the easiest and quickest of canyon putts, but also bears the most traffic as the main thoroughfare between the Valley and Malibu. The 2- to 4-lane highway offers scenic pockets as it borders state parks, and passes by some interesting dwellings. To get to the Rock Store, turn north onto Mullholland Highway.

Latigo Canyon- Not for acrophobiacs, Latigo Canyon is an awesome rim route through one of the steeper canyons. The hills tumble into the sea as you climb away from the coast and is National Geographic material, but don't get too mesmerized as there are no guard rails. As you go deeper into the canyon, the road gets more nestled into the terrain, but is always a tight ride with challenging twists and climbs. The scenery is a blend of estates and the architectural marvels of Buckminister Fuller prodigies. You can get to the Rock Store by turning east on Kanan Dume and then south again on Mullholland Highway.

Kanan Dume- This 4-lane highway is more scenic and isolated than Malibu Canyon, but not as challenging as the smaller canyon routes. Long, sweeping curves constitute most of the trip over the mountains. Sculptured rock formations and wide-angle views of soft mountain peaks highlight this route. You can reach the Rock Store off Kanan Dume by turning south onto Mullholland Highway and downshifting through the twisting descent to the Rock Store's front door.

Decker and Encinal Canyons- Both these routes are short, steep and fun little jaunts off Mullholland Highway down to the Pacific Coast Highway. You'll feel like a cowboy or gal riding through a chaparral trail in the sticks. Although the roads seem very remote, local residential traffic into the glamour homes is sometimes heavy. Both alternate routes are west off Mullholland Highway.

Portero Road- For benders who can't leave the saddle, this countryish back road will take you all the way to Camarillo in Ventura County. Portero Road links up with Decker Canyon Road east of Mullholland Highway. There's a tricky right turn at Newbury Park to continue on Portero Road. If you end up on Hwy. 101 in a mile or so from the turn, you missed it. Try again, because this pleasant run through grassy fields ascending to panoramic views is a real breather from the Los Angeles basin and a time warp back to a more sedate California.

In Camarillo, Portero Road intersects Los Posas Road where a left turn will lead to the Pacific Coast Highway, south. (See Pacific Coast Highway Tour.) And a right turn will lead to Hwy. 101, south, toward San Fernando Valley and Los Angeles.

Sagebrush Cantina, 23527 Calabasas Road, (off Calabasas Parkway exit from Hwy. 101 or between Topanga Canyon and Las Virgines from the coast), is a destination many bikers look forward to when riding the Santa Monica hills. Big Screen T.V.'s, indoor and outdoor stages featuring live entertainment and fishbowl margaritas with Mexican food draw a partying crowd throughout the day on weekends.

Mullholland Drive- The southern stretch of Mullholland on the south side of Topanga State Park travels the ridge in the hills separating San Fernando Valley and Los Angeles. It can be reached off **Sepulveda Boulevard** which follows I-405 south. Mullholland Drive is a pretty ride but is also heavily travelled by commuters as a freeway alternative during peak traffic hours.

Once known for auto racing with the wagering of pink slips, this part of the "Mul" has twists, dips, and vertical drops into the canyon where rusted out cars from the days of drag racing still lie. Today, homes have taken over the hills, but there are grassy fields or lovers' pullouts where you can soak in the spectacular views of both valleys.

If you take Mullholland Drive to get to Mullholland Highway, the Drive will run into Fwy. 405, north. Take Fwy. 405 to Hwy. 101, toward Ventura, and exit at Topanga Canyon Boulevard, west, to reach Mullholland Highway. Exit at Parkway Calabasas to reach the Sagebrush Cantina.

At the end of the day if you're on the Pacific Coast Highway with the majority of Angelinos, your clutch hand aching and splitting lanes seems futile, there is an alternative route. **Sunset Boulevard** will wind you up to I-405. The 4-lane boulevard cuts through the ritzy Westside, but for some reason the road is always impoverished by potholes. Use caution as you round turns on the residential strip as you don't want to flip into someone's gated estate with hungry guard dogs waiting.

MULLHOLLAND HIGHWAY HIGHLIGHTS

Approximate Mileage: 100 miles roundtrip from Los Angeles

Road Ratings:
MULLHOLLAND HIGHWAY/ SLABBER; 2-lane, good pavement, scenic,
    some twists.
MULLHOLLAND DRIVE/ BENDER; 2-lane, scenic, twists, traffic.
TOPANGA CANYON/ MEANDERER; 2-lane, good pavement, curves.
OLD TOPANGA ROAD/ BENDER; 2-lane narrow, twists, scenic.
MALIBU CANYON/ MEANDERER; 2 - 4 lane, curves, traffic, scenic
    pockets, good pavement.
KANAN DUME/ MEANDERER; 2 - 4 lane, curves, scenic, good pavement.
LATIGO CANYON/ BENDER; 2-lane narrow, steep, tight curves, scenic.
DECKER & ENCINAL CANYONS/ BENDER; 2-lane, steep, scenic, curves,
    watch pavement conditions.
PORTERO ROAD/ MEANDERER; 2-lane, winding with curves, climbs,
    scenic, good pavement.

Weather:
Dress in layers except on very hot days. Conditions range in the
canyons from cool breezes throughout the year on the ocean side of
mountain range to hot in summer and cold in winter on the valley
side. Ridge winds are also common.

Restaurants:
Rock Store, Mullholland Highway, between Las Virgenes and Kanan
    Dume Road, (818) 889-1311.
Sagebrush Cantina, 23527 Calabasas Rd., Calabasas. (818) 222-6062
Neptune's Net, 42505 Pacific Coast Hwy. at County Line.

Attractions:
Malibu Creek State Park   Paramount Ranch

Local Harley-Davidson Dealers:
BARGER HARLEY-DAVIDSON, 22107 Sherman Way, Canoga Park,
    (818) 999-3355
BARTEL'S HARLEY-DAVIDSON, 4141 Lincoln Blvd., Marina Del Rey,
    (310) 823-1112
VAN NUYS HARLEY-DAVIDSON, 7630 Van Nuys Blvd., Van Nuys,
    (818) 989-2230

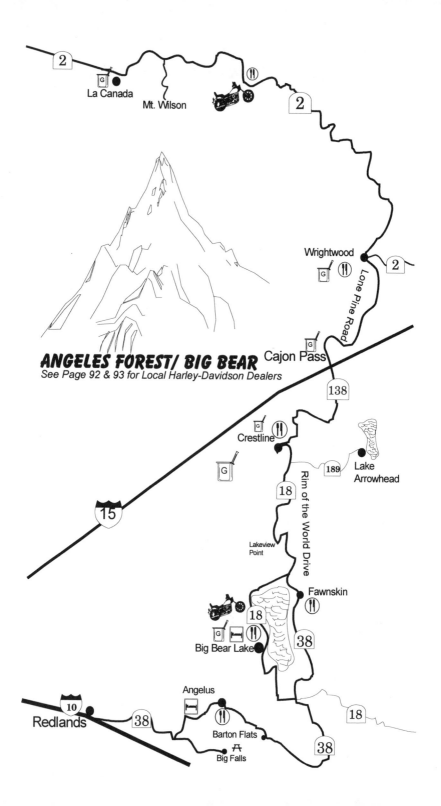

2 — La Canada

G

Mt. Wilson

2

2 — Wrightwood

G

Lone Pine Road

G — Cajon Pass

ANGELES FOREST/ BIG BEAR
See Page 92 & 93 for Local Harley-Davidson Dealers

138

15

Crestline

G

G

18

189 — Lake Arrowhead

Rim of the World Drive

Lakeview Point

Fawnskin

18

38

Big Bear Lake

G

10 — Redlands

38

Angelus

Barton Flats

Big Falls

18

38

ANGELES FOREST / BIG BEAR

Are you daring enough to get intimate on such curvaceous and appealing road that you might divorce yourself from nagging reality? This road affair is on those humps to the north— the San Gabriel and San Bernardino Mountains.

The dual range ridge run with altitudes ranging from 1,300 to 8,400 feet is only open spring through fall. In the Angeles Forest, Hwy. 2's loose curves lend to a rhythmic sprint over its piney crest and drops down to Cajon Pass. In the San Bernardino Forest, you'll literally ride the Rim of the World, a scenic trail along the length of the range.

Another liberating aspect of this tour is its direct line of travel. You can leave the map under the saddle as there is no complex route to follow. You can give undivided attention to the curves and scenery.

Hwy. 2, Angeles Forest Highway, is located off Fwy. 2 which intersects I-5 and I-210. Take the La Canada/ Flintridge exit and make a left into the Angeles Forest. Gas is just off the exit and is the last opportunity until the other side of the forest, about 60 miles.

The police, staked out at the base of the mountain with tow truck in tow, pounce on speed demons testing their bikes' limits. Those without a motorcycle license, might have their bikes impounded on location.

Once civilization is at your back, set the throttle and go for it up the incline into the forest. When John Muir discovered this patch of wilderness, he marvelled over its hills of honey bloom.

There are no critical turns at first, and you can easily keep your speed up to 40 - 50 mph as you start to climb into the pines. You'll ride the granite rim of the mountain, with city views diminishing until your wheels are well nestled into the back hills, enjoying fine pavement.

The Mt. Wilson turnoff is about the only diversion you might consider in the Angeles Forest. Unless it's a Mr. Clean day in the basin or you're into astronomy, the narrow winding road with some critical turns to the observatory will probably not be worth the extra time. However, on a clear day from this vantage point you can see all of Southern California, including Catalina Island.

Back to Hwy. 2, crotch rockets who alluded police will be buzzing by until you hit Newcomb's Ranch, about 25 miles from the base. In this stretch avoid riding close to the center line, and ride within your means for your own safety. While on the topic of safety, beware of rockslides. Be particularly observant around cliffs on narrow bends.

Newcomb's Ranch is a pit stop for motorcyclists, particularly those on speedy imports—hawgs are in the minority here. The woodsy, rustic bar and restaurant has an ample fireplace for warming up on cold days.

Continuing on Hwy. 2, the road will begin to follow the crest. You'll think you've reached heaven when you meet a St. Peter's eye view from the desert to the sea. The vast desert floor fills the north side view from the ridge. On the south, an echo of mountain ranges starts out in perspective with verdant detail, extending to a sharp, purply silhouette in the distance.

When the road starts to straighten out after Big Pines, you've reached Swarthout Valley and the small town of *Wrightwood*. It's a pleasant walking village with cafes and little shops.

After Wrightwood, Hwy. 2 will continue to the northeast, but you'll want to make a right turn on **Lone Pine Road** to cross over the Cajon Pass and hop on Hwy. 138 to Big Bear.

Lone Pine Road is a desolate descent out of the burnt siena hills into rustic Cajon Pass. Before you reach bottom, you'll probably hear a gasp from a fellow rider, even over the roar of engines. They've come out over the crest to the breathtaking view of Mormon Rocks, an inanimate cluster of natural beauty.

At the I-15 junction there is gas and a snack shop. In the time it takes to finish a bag of chips, a train will undoubtedly clack by. About 60 freight and passenger trains roll by on these tracks daily.

Riders south of Los Angeles in San Bernardino, Riverside, Orange and San Diego counties can enter the Pass from I-15 and ride either or both ranges from this mid-entry point. Exit I-15 at **Hwy. 138**.

Continuing across I-15 on Lone Pine Road, it will automatically become Hwy. 138 and begin to curl up into the San Bernardino Mountain Range. The road is like a bobsled run on wheels, naturally carved from the terrain as it goes up, down, and around the trees and icy fresh lakes.

Unlike the Angeles Forest, there are residential pockets throughout these mountains. People do come and go out of the driveways along the road.

After the town of Crestline, where food and gas are available, the road will become **Hwy. 18, Rim of the World Drive**. It hugs the forested cliffs with a view of the sprawl connecting San Bernardino and Riverside Counties.

Before reaching Big Bear Lake, look for *Lakeview Point.* This vantage point will let you examine the twists and turns in the upcoming road that leads to the head of Bear Valley and the popular recreational lake.

Upon entering the valley, there are two travel options. Hwy. 18 leads to the town of Big Bear Lake and is the more populated side. On the main drag is a popular motorcycle hangout, Chad's Place, serving up a biker bill of fare and of course, it's equipped with a bar. If you want to spend the night, Big Bear Lake has over 30 resorts, ranging from funky cabins to posh hotels.

Hwy. 18 wraps around to the other side of the lake and drops down into Lucerne Valley, linking up to Hwy. 247 to Pioneer Town and Joshua Tree. (See Joshua Tree Tour.) One would think the desert side would be warmer, but often it's not. Even at midday in May temperatures can be in the low 50's. Hwy. 18 in this area also has critical turn pockets past Baldwin Lake on Cushenbury Grade.

Hwy. 38 will take you to the less populated side of the lake and the little resort town of Fawnskin, then crosses Hwy. 18 and drops down to the San Bernardino basin to all the major freeways.

Before worrying about slabbing home, there are more scenic stops to prolong the magical mountain tour. Climbing out of Bear Valley on Hwy. 38, you'll reach Onyx Summit at 8400 feet. Crawl through the summit to enjoy the view of San Gorgonio, its 11,000-foot peak usually remains snow capped throughout the year.

The road is in good condition and there are no turns that require a down shift to less than 25-mph, however because there is infrequent traffic on this route, you might encounter a deer crossing the road.

There are scenic small towns along the way. Barton Flats has an out of the way loop along Jenks Lake. There are other side roads in the area, such as to Sugarloaf Mountain and Holcomb Valley, but most become dirt and gravel along the way or require river forging at some point.

If you're looking to kill some time or want to relive school day field trips, visit the Tourist Information Center and Ranger Station in Barton Flats. In addition to the displays on local flora and fauna they also have a "road kill" petting zoo. Along a fence are all the pelts of the little varmits that often end up under your wheel.

In the town of Seven Oaks, off Glass Road, there is a little lodge with a zoo and general store that can serve as a pit stop. To inquire about rooms in the lodge call (909) 794-1277. You can also camp in the comfort of cabins here and take a dip in the swimming hole.

Angelus Oaks is another scenic side stop with *The Oaks* restaurant, known for serving up tasty meals. A great place to walk them off in the great out-doors is *Big Falls*, located off Hwy. 38 on the **Forest Falls** turnoff five miles from town.

If you've got the energy, turn your biking boots into hiking boots and take the 1/2-mile easy trek to the cascading waters. The tiered water fall is a rare treat, and you can enjoy it even longer by camping or picnicking at this out of the way spot.

All good things will end at the intersection of **Orange Street** where Hwy. 38, also called Mill Creek Road, will cease to exist shortly after the town of Mentone. A left will lead to **I-10** where you can link up to other freeways to super slab home or on to the next great adventure. (See Joshua Tree or Anza - Borrego Tours.)

ANGELES FOREST/ BIG BEAR HIGHLIGHTS

Approximate Mileage: 190 miles round trip from Los Angeles

Road Ratings:
Fwy. 2/ SLABBER; multi-lane, usually light traffic.
Hwy. 2/ MEANDERER; 2 - 4 lane, mountainous, scenic, mini landslides.
LONE PINE ROAD/ SLABBER; 2-lane, isolated, good pavement.
Hwy. 138/ MEANDERER; 2 - 4 lane, scenic, mountainous twists and
      curves, residential.
Hwy. 18 (RIM OF THE WORLD DRIVE)/ MEANDERER; scenic, mountainous,
twists on backside into Lucerne Valley.
Hwy. 38/ MEANDERER; 2-lane, curves, mountainous, isolated, deer.
I-10/ SLABBER; multi-lane, congested, connects to other freeways.

Road Conditions:
California Highway Patrol 1-800-427-7623

Weather:
Hwy. 2 from Mt. Waterman to Wrightwood is closed during snowy
season. Warm during day in summer season, but temperature drops
quickly at sunset. Cool in fall and spring. Cool at high altitudes.

Restaurants:
Newcomb's Ranch, Hwy. 2, Mt. Waterman. (818) 440-1001
Chad's, 4740 Village Dr., Big Bear. (909) 866-2161
Oaks Cafe, Angelus Oaks

Accommodations:
Big Bear Reservations (909) 866-5753
Seven Oaks Mountain Cabins (909) 794-1277

Attractions:
Lakeview Point Big Falls

Local Harley-Davidson Dealers:
QUAID HARLEY-DAVIDSON, 25160 Redlands Blvd., Loma Linda
      (909) 796-8399
HARLEY-DAVIDSON OF GLENDALE, 3717 San Fernando Rd., Glendale,
      (818) 246-5618
LAIDLAW'S HARLEY-DAVIDSON, 8351 E. Garvey Blvd., Rosemead,
      (818) 280-3977

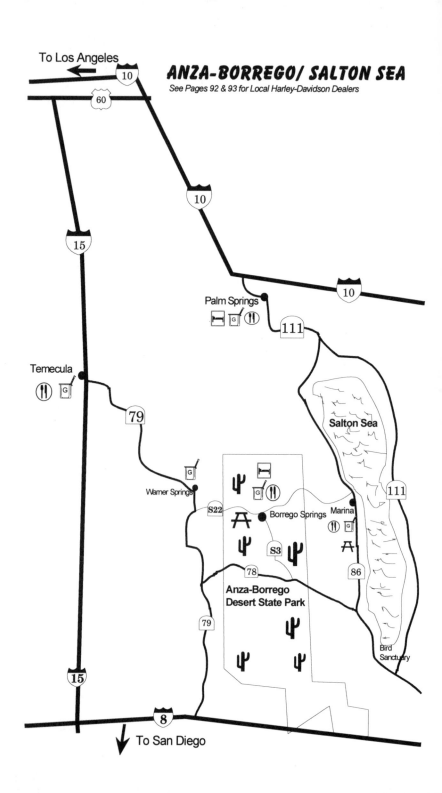

ANZA-BORREGO/ SALTON SEA

Whether you're a weekend slabber or a bender never out of the saddle, you'll enjoy this trek into the California southern desert, particularly in springtime. Blooming cactus, badlands, sparkling air, and snow-capped mountains await you at the southern end of the state. You can always camp or get a hotel room if you're building up to a full day of riding.

Despite the extreme heat and cold conditions in the desert, these roads are good and the pavement is maintained. However, temperature might be a consideration for comfort, and although the terrain is an interesting ride throughout the year, it can be biting cold in winter and blistering hot in summer. Check the weather for the southern desert during the time you wish to ride.

Anza-Borrego has a total of 600,000 acres. Getting your bearings on the first visit might become confusing. There are four paved roads with mile markers that you can use as a guide along with tour maps available at the entrance kiosks and visitor centers. In addition to the paved roads there are 500 more miles of dirt road that you can inquire about. We'll be staying on the paved roads.

From the San Diego area, take scenic **Hwy. 78** through the orchards toward Julian. (See South San Diego Tour.) In this old mining town you can gas up and take a riding break for breakfast or for a cup of coffee and an apple fritter.

Slabbers can continue on Hwy. 78 directly into the park and link up with **S3**. Benders might prefer to add riding miles by taking Hwy. 78 to **S2** near Scissor Crossing and then continue north at the junction through San Felipe Valley, the route of the historic Butterfield Stagecoach. The junction got its name from the quarter-mile jog in County Road S2 to cross San Felipe Creek, resembling scissor blades on a road map. Continue on S2 to **S22** and Rancherita. You'll enter the park at its northern end as described by arrival from the Los Angeles area.

From Los Angeles, Orange, Riverside or San Bernardino Counties, take **Fwy. 91** toward Corona, and then south on **I-15** to Temecula. The little resort town, popular for wine tasting, hot air ballooning, and antique shopping has a quaint downtown area with old western storefronts. You'll find a variety of cafes and restaurants in the older part of town. If you make Temecula by breakfast, try the *Swing Inn* for a hearty country meal.

Continuing south through Temecula's downtown, link up with **Hwy. 79**, south. This stretch is 38 miles of scenic valley with ranches and wineries. The 2-lane road will become hilly and climb into chaparral, with the valley on one side and Mt. Palomar chaperoning the ride on the other. The road is a pleasant run with curves, dips, and ample opportunity for passing entourages on their way to Anza-Borrego.

In the town of *Warner Springs,* gas is available. Approximately 5 miles past town, take the **S-2** turnoff, east, a climb up a short hill to **S-22**. A posted sign indicates that a left turn toward Borrego Springs/ Rancherita will keep you on S-22.

A world of wonderful twists and turns will drop 2500 feet into *Anza-Borrego Desert State Park*. Use turnouts for soaking up the panorama views, so you don't otherwise Evil Knievel into the sea of prickly plants on the desert floor. The body of water 30-miles in the distance is the Salton Sea. At the entry kiosk for Anza-Borrego, there is a small fee for motorcycles to enter the park.

S-22 becomes **Palm Canyon Road** and leads to the resort town of *Borrego Springs* with gas, restaurants, and hotels. A popular and inexpensive restaurant in town for raved-about Mexican food is Mi Tenapa. (However, it's more fun to eat in the Salton Sea Marina.) If you're saddle sore or interested in snooping one of the country's largest parks, hotels are listed in the highlights section.

There really isn't a lot to do in Anza-Borrego's resort community other than be a pool lizard by day and a stargazer by night. A visitor's center near Borrego Springs has literature that describe the various sights and rides.

Continuing on S-22 toward Salton Sea, the ride through the Park displays a variety of desert landscapes—perfect alluvial fan formations from eroding hills and miniature versions of badlands. In spring, the muted desert floor blooms with color from blooming succulents and wild flowers. People journey from all over the world to see Anza-Borrego during this season.

Off the road, there are several overlooks where you can stop and have a nature stretch. Portions of most walking trails are even accessible by biker boot. *Smoketree Overlook* located .4 miles from mile-marker 34 has a patch of Smoketrees to wander in and is an ideal spot to admire the desert wildflowers if in bloom. The spidery plant growing everywhere is called Ocotillo.

Outside the park, the road continues to Salton Sea, and its isolation will lure you into breaking the sound barrier. Don't forget to pre-check your insurance coverage and DMV record before engaging in such fatalistic thrill.

When you get to the junction of **Hwy. 86**, continue ahead a few miles into the community of *Salton Sea* where you'll find the "marina" to your right and the lost-in-time *Tiki Restaurant*. Not quite at par with modern marinas, Salton Sea has a mystique all its own, best described as Alfred Hitchcock meets Monty Python.

The area was a dried up lake bed until 1905 when the Colorado River flooded into its basin. The 2-year overflow was due to the irrigation blunder of Charles Rockwood and his first attempt to convert the Imperial Valley into the rich agricultural land it eventually became. The Salton Sea developed into a 14-mile wide gigantic inland sea. It's about 235 feet below sea level.

In the 1950's there was an attempt to turn the area into a resort but that was blundered too, and it left the eerie, partly developed settlement of today with its streets leading to nowhere. The Sea itself adds to the strange ambiance and aromatherapy when its exotic creatures occasionaly die in clusters along the shore.

Retirees mostly populate the region. There is gas (3 miles from the Tiki Restaurant), markets, and bars. If you find it hard to tear yourself away, Hwy. 86 links up with **Hwy. 111** on the other side of the sea for more exploring. Scattered along the shore, you'll find mom & pop motels, restaurants, and bars.

At the southern end of the sea, off Hwy. 111, there is a Wildlife Refuge where you can eyeball a variety of migratory birds that use the sea as an inland aquatic pit stop.

You can depart the area via

the same scenic route or super slab your way through Indio and Palm Springs to **I-10** and use Fwy. 91 or Fwy 60.

Alternate routes off **Hwy. 111** to **Hwy. 74** will take you on a breathtaking climb into Idyllwild where you can cool off in summer or throw snowballs in winter.

For additional riding alternatives in Anza-Borrego, take **S-3** from Borrego Springs, also called Yaqui Pass to **Hwy. 78**, east, and link up to Hwy. 86 to get to Salton Sea. This route will add 25 more scenic miles of park riding. Overlooks from the road will give you spectacular views as you climb to 1200-foot elevations.

To return to the San Diego area take **Hwy. 86**, south, or Hwy. 111, south, near Salton Sea to **I-8**, west, and the scenic Jacumba Pass. (See South San Diego Tour).

You can get to northern San Diego County by taking **Hwy. 78**, west, and ride the country backroad toward Julian for more apple cider, apple pie, and apple T-shirts. Continuing on Hwy. 78 leads to Oceanside where you can link up with I-5 and slab home.

Benders heading toward Orange or Los Angeles Counties can gamble their stamina by exiting off the freeway to **Hwy.**

1 at San Clemente or Dana Point. (See PCH Tour South.)

To return to Los Angeles, Riverside, or San Bernardino County, take **Hwy. 111**, north, from Salton Sea and link up with I-10 or Fwy. 60.

ANZA-BORREGO/ SALTON SEA HIGHLIGHTS

Approximate Mileage: 340 miles round trip from Los Angeles

Road Ratings:
Hwy. 79/ MEANDERER; scenic, winding, good pavement.
S-2/ BENDER; 2-lane, climbing, winding, views, good pavement.
S-22/ MEANDERER; 2-lane, riding variety, good pavement, scenic.
Hwy 78/ MEANDERER; 2-lane, scenic, riding variety.
Hwy. 86/ SLABBER; 2-lane, good pavement.
Hwy. 111/ SLABBER; 2-lane, good pavement.

Weather:
Hot in summer, cold in winter with unpredictable rain and floods.
Layers or jackets suggested in spring and fall. Carry water.

Restaurants:
Swing Inn, 28676 Front St., Temecula. (909) 676-2321
Salton Tiki Restaurant, Salton Sea Marina, Salton Sea.
    (760) 395-2066

Accommodations:
Guest House Inn, Temecula, spa, restaurant. (909) 676-5700
Doubletree Suites, Temecula, full amenities. (909) 676-5656
Oasis Motel, Borrego Springs, spa. (760) 767-5409
Palm Canyon Resort, Borrego Springs. (760) 767-5341

Attractions:
Temecula Old Town
Anza-Borrego State Park
Salton Sea and Wildlife Refuge

Local Harley-Davidson Dealer:
HARLEY-DAVIDSON OF EL CAJON, 621 El Cajon Blvd., El Cajon,
    (619) 444-1123
SOUTH COAST HARLEY-DAVIDSON, 345 E Street, San Diego, Chula
    Vista, (619) 420-7000
PALM SPRINGS HARLEY-DAVIDSON, 19465 N. Indian, North Palm
    Springs, (760) 329-1448

ORTEGA HIGHWAY/ SAN JACINTO MOUNTAINS

See Pages 92 & 93 for Local Harley-Davidson Dealers

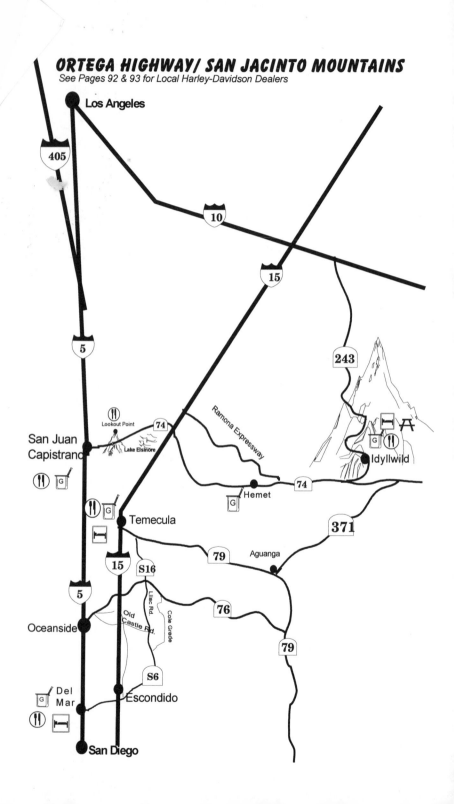

ORTEGA HIGHWAY/ SAN JACINTO MOUNTAINS

If you've always wanted to be a contender, this is the road to test riding skill and stamina. The 250-mile, lasso-shaped tour southeast of Los Angeles might not appear challenging by map, but you'll be sharing the turf with crotch rockets. If you're in the mood for a leisurely putt, pick another route. But if you want to ride with the Tasmanian dare devils on wheels, come prepared with good nerves, a tight grip, and an extensive vocabulary of four-letter words.

If you survive the threat of road kill, (Otega Highway has a pernicious reputation, being several riders' last ride,) some areas are so nice you might want to spend the night. The San Jacinto Mountains are a convenient and relaxing Alpine getaway.

Hop on any freeway that will get you to **I-5**, and continue on to Orange County. This commute always seems congested. You can avoid traffic by leaving early in the morning on weekends. From the north, you'll pass through Irvine, Laguna Niguel, and Mission Viejo to San Juan Capistrano and the **Hwy. 74** exit. From the south, start looking for Hwy. 74 after the town of San Clemente. By heading east on Hwy. 74, you're immediately on **Ortega Highway**.

However, if you're in the need of breakfast, lunch, or a leg stretch, a pleasant pit stop is just west off the exit in San Juan Capistrano near the Capistrano Mission. On the right before the mission, there is *Walnut Grove Restaurant*, satisfying locals and travellers for 50 years with its home cooking and fresh baked goods.

Down Camino Capistrano, the main street from the Mission, there are cafes and souvenir shops filled with Indian crafts and '40s and '50s collectibles. If you arrive later in the morning, the iron horses should be starting to line up outside the *Swallows Inn*, a country-western bar serving burgers and Mexican food.

Ortega Highway is a 30-mile scenic canyon run that ascends into *Caspers Regional ark* and the Cleveland National Forest. Although you might be riding with a buddy, the headlight you see filling your rear view mirror is probably not his or hers. And when it passes you on a blind curve at 65 mph you can be sure it's a crotch rocket.

It's wise to stay away from the center line—even the double striped sections get no respect in the area. After rains, water and slides are other road conditions to watch for on the highway. There is a snack shop at the top of the mountain, *The Lookout*, where you can quench a thirst, curb an appetite, relish a view, and settle nerves.

Continuing down the mountain, Lake Elsinore will appear, and you'll want to go through the '50s, sleepy community toward **I-15**. Go south 15 miles to *Temecula,* also a good place for a riding break. Its Western-style Old Town along Front Street has cafes and antique shops. Exit from I-15 or continue by freeway to link up with **Hwy. 79**, a beauty of a back road ride into Aguanga. Just past Aguanga you'll come to the beginning of **Hwy. 371**, which heads northeast toward Indio. The road begins the climb to Santa Rosa Summit at 4,900 feet. On a clear day you'll swear that you can see to Maui.

There are a couple of small towns that break up the open road and provide gas.

The highway deadends into **Hwy. 74**, about 50 miles from Temecula. Go left onto Hwy. 74 for 30 miles of riding enjoyment through pine forest and Ponderosa-like ranch spreads on open ranges. At Mountain Center, make a right onto **Hwy. 243** toward Idyllwild.

Climbing and weaving up the San Jacinto Mountains will lead to Idyllwild, a picturesque, Alpine village with gas, restaurants, and strolling. It's a popular getaway, and spending the night usually requires reservations with two-night stays on weekends.

Looping back west on Hwy. 74 from Idyllwild, the road drops down the mountain into the agricultural San Jacinto basin. Before reaching the town of Hemet, look for the **Ramona Expressway** if you'd like to ride open country without interruption. It's a nice transition from the mountain twisties and the inevitable slabbing to return home.

By knowing who Ramona was, you can also impress a riding companion along this pastoral but pungent run through cattle land. The expressway honors the legend of a novel character authored by Helen Hunt Jackson. Based on a California-slanted Romeo and Juliet, Ramona and her lover of Indian blood roamed this territory in search of a home where their interracial marriage would be accepted. However, the couple only encountered grief and the eventual death of Ramona's hubby.

So enamored is the population of the story, an annual pageant featuring Ramona still takes place in Hemet. When riding through the San Diego region, you'll find other landmarks pertaining to the story, including the town of Ramona near Julian.

Ramona Expressway will intersect with Hwy. 215 and become **Cajalco Road,** a pleasant, curving run with an alien atmosphere of intriguing rocks. You'll have 15 miles of peaceful riding enjoyment before the grind of **I-15** appears at Lake Matthews. Link up with **Hwy. 91** to continue toward Los Angeles. You should be back well in time for the 8 o'clock movie.

If you don't give a damn about a movie, there's plenty more riding routes to explore in the area. On **Hwy. 79**, a half mile east of Temecula, take **S16** to **Hwy. 76**. This tucked-away stretch runs along a stream and provides a variety of terrain to enjoy from lush meadows to jagged cliffs. You'll also pass through the Pala Indian Reservation and Mission San Antonio de Pala. At the junction with Hwy. 76 there is a small market for provisions.

Take **Hwy. 76** east, onto Cole Grade. It will be a memorable right turn into the old days of Southern California as you ride through acres of avocado and orange groves. The road will ascend for a bird's eye view of the neat rows of crops. At **S6,** you'll want to make a right.

S6 will take you into Escondido, or for more adventure turn right at **Lilac Road** to **Old Castle Road** and veer left. More curves and views await, including a car museum and the Deer Park Winery, but the most exciting aspect of your journey will be linking up with Champagne Road and the Lawrence Welk Resort! Did you forget your golf clubs and dancing shoes? You can always stop for a time-share tour or souvenir.

Continuing on S6 southwest, you'll discover an enjoyable route to the Pacific Ocean. Picturesque horse ranches and Lake Hodges are some of the scenic pleasantries as you

,ide through eucalyptus groves splintering the road with their lanky shadows.

S6 will take you into the seaside community of Del Mar. Make a left at the ocean and follow the signs to the Amtrak station where you'll be rewarded with seaside restaurants right on the sand. Take off your boots and dig your toes into the warm grains. The *Poseidon* is a favorite spot with good food as well as ambiance.

Along the coast highway, you'll find more restaurants, as well as hotels if you're in need of an Ibuprofin, bath, and bed. Del Mar is one of the more posh areas to vacation in. Farther north on the coast highway you'll find slightly less resorty beach communities such as Solana Beach, Cardiff, Encinitas, Leucadia, and Carlsbad. Along this recreational stretch you should encounter at least one establishment with a row of bikes outside its doors.

ORTEGA HIGHWAY/ IDYLLWILD HIGHLIGHTS

Approximate Mileage: 250 miles round trip from Los Angeles

Road Ratings:
HWY. 74/ MEANDERER; 2-lane, scenic, riding variety.
I-15/ SLABBER; multi-lane freeway, scenic, generally light traffic.
HWY. 79/ MEANDERER; 2-lane, scenic, climbing.
HWY. 371/ MEANDERER; 2-lane, remote, scenic.

Weather:
Coastal climate in Capistrano, higher temperatures inland, and cool temperatures at higher elevations. Snow in winter in Idyllwild. Dress in layers all year round.

Restaurants:
Swallows Inn, 31786 Camino Capistrano, Capistrano. (949) 493-3188
Walnut Grove, 26871 Ortega Highway, Capistrano.
The Lookout, Hwy. 74 at summit.
Temecula, see Anza-Borrego Tour Highlights
Jan's Red Kettle, 54220 N. Circle Drive, Idyllwild; local's spot.
Poseiden, across from Amtrak station, Del Mar.

Accommodations:
Knotty Pine Cabins, Idyllwild; furnished cabins with fireplaces and kitchens in conifer grove. (909) 659-2933.
Woodland Park Manor, Idyllwild; located in village center, pool, 2-night minimum on weekends. (909) 659-2657.
Del Mar Inn, Del Mar, near ocean, gardens and spa. (619) 755-9765.

Attractions:
Capistrano	The Lookout scenic point
Old Town, Temecula	Idyllwild

Local Harley-Davidson Dealers:
HARLEY'S HOUSE OF HARLEYS, 1555 S. Coast Hwy., Oceanside,
    800-4-HARLEY & (760) 433-2060
QUAID TEMECULA HARLEY-DAVIDSON, 28822 Front St. Temecula,
    (909) 506-6903
PALM SPRINGS HARLEY-DAVIDSON, 19465 N. Indian, North Palm Springs,
    (760) 329-1448

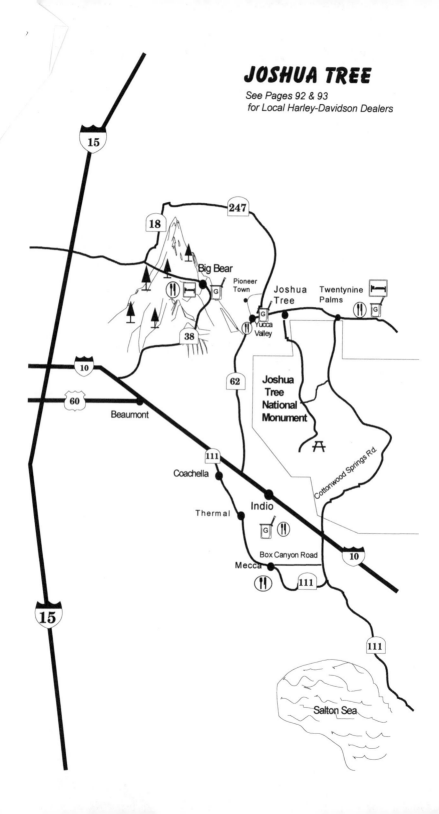

JOSHUA TREE

If you like those good, good slabbing vibrations, a trip to Joshua Tree is right up your fast lane. The 340-mile round trip ride from Los Angeles is 250 highway miles and 90-plus sightseeing miles in one of California's most spectacular deserts.

Like Anza-Borrego, Joshua Tree is magnificent in the spring after a rainy winter when the colorful wildflowers sprout from the stark desert vase. Bring a camera along to capture the desert in springtime.

Any time of year, the desert displays a distinctive character to the season. Joshua Tree offers a variety of pristine desert landscapes and the unusual formations of its namesake tree, which is actually part of the lily family. Prepare a lunch at home or buy one along the way for picnicing inside the park. There are no snack stands or restaurants.

In the winter, as with the other rides, you can expect coolish temperatures and unpredictable rains. Riding in the desert might be very pleasant when other areas of Southern California are not weather perfect.

Temperatures soar in summer, so leave the heavy leather at home if you don't want to dehydrate into giant-size jerky. Not far from Joshua Tree is the town of Thermal, where the country's daily highs are routinely recorded during the summer. Fall and spring are generally the preferred seasons for comfortable riding.

From the San Diego area, take **I-15,** north, to **Fwy. 60**, east, or connect from the Ortega Highway or South San Diego Tours. From Los Angeles, Orange, Riverside, or San Bernardino counties take either **Fwy. 91**, east, or **Fwy. 60**, east, to **I-10**, east. Fwy. 60 through the Moreno Valley area (before it links up with I-10) is a pretty canyon run that breaks up the endless suburb sea with scenic open territory as you cross Los Angeles and Riverside Counties. Along I-10, traditional truck stops and cafes that look like country homes periodically appear on the north side of the frontage road.

There are three entrances into Joshua Tree National Park. We recommend the one 23 miles east of Indio. There are gas stations all the way from Los Angeles to Indio, but after that the next fuel stop is 75 miles away in the town of Joshua Tree, outside the park.

Although there are several entrances into the park, the one past Indio will keep the usual 25 to 30 mph winds at your back. Riders find the winds crossing I-10 near Hwy. 62 in the lower desert are often fighting to dictate which way a bike should go. If you're concerned, call the California Highway Patrol or Joshua Tree Park Service to check wind advisories before venturing off.

This southerly entry also allows more riding miles in the park. There is a nominal entrance fee to enter Joshua Tree National Park. For literature describing the variety of scenic tours and spots within the national park, stop at the Cottonwood Visitor Center. Brochures will also describe the indigenous plants of the region including the variety of cactuses, yuccas, and flowers.

The park roads are posted 45 mph and are clean, well-maintained, and fun to ride. The curves are heaven-sent after the rigid freeway run.

If you don't stop for brochures at the visitor centers, take time to stop at the vista points and conveniently located exhibits, indicated by the international signs along the road. They convey information on the valleys that start at about 3,000 feet above sea level to the granite peaks at 6,000 feet.

The selection of side roads are few, and about the only one that remains within park boundaries is the 4-mile, must-see road to Keyes View, with a memorable panorama from a 5,000-ft vantage point. Jumbo Rocks is another attraction off this road.

Back to the main park road, continue on until the first picnic area, Hidden Valley, and pull in for lunch or at least to take the short nature hike through the massive boulders. Like just about any big cluster of boulders in California, these were also used as a hideout for rustlers wanted by the law or lynch mob.

Continuing through the park, there are more points of interest to explore before exiting onto **Hwy. 62,** leading to Joshua Tree, Twentynine Palms and the town of Yucca Valley.

These desert towns are growing communities and extend a warm welcome to the motorcycling set. The new *Super 8* motel in the town of Yucca Valley even offers a biker's discount.

One place where you will see a line-up of bikes in the early afternoon is at *Hutchins Harley-Davidson Route 62 Diner,* located next door to the dealership. It's a popular pit stop with bikers for breakfast, lunch, or afternoon refreshments with a menu that specifically caters to hungry riders.

If you wish to spend more time in the area or use the trip as a springboard for more touring, there are also inexpensive accommodations in Twentynine Palms, including a few authentic adobe abodes.

K-B Ranchotel is a landmark bed and breakfast, and the innkeepers are very biker friendly. They'll invite you into their living room for a chat and homemade snack, while you watch piranha swim in a swampy aquarium. (See the Highlights Section.)

To return home via I-10, ride south on Hwy. 62, a scenic trail through austere Morengo Valley. For meanderers and benders, the area does offer more riding and entertainment.

Off Hwy. 62, **Pioneer Road** to *Pioneer Town* is a fun loop to explore. The town is the remains of a movie set rather than mining town. Cowboy actors Roy Rogers and Gene Autry helped finance the development of the authentic looking western town built in the 1940s. The set design included full structures rather than facades most commonly used in those days at the movie studios. You can almost hear the spurs clicking on the sidewalk or the hoofs of a posse riding out of town, as you stroll down its once cinematic strip.

Today the town is inhabited by wanna-be cowboys and gals who look forward to weekend line dancing at *Pappy & Harriet's.* The town saloon and restaurant, is open Wednesday through Sunday, its mesquite grill sizzling away in a festive, country-western atmosphere. If you dance your pretty little boots off at P&H's, Pioneer Town Motel awaits with 12 rooms for the first lucky parties to register. (See Highlights Section.)

Pioneer Road loops back to Hwy. 62 or links with **Hwy. 247.** By continuing northeast, it will connect with Hwy. 18, the back way into Big Bear. (See Angeles Forest/ Big Bear Tour).

Continuing on Hwy. 62 to the east, it will connect to **Hwy.**

95, north, to **Hwy. 163** toward Laughlin and the Colorado River. Benders can continue on Hwy. 95 to the lights of Las Vegas, but will probably have to call it a day and find a room on the strip.

A side journey on the way to Joshua Tree that will relieve you a little earlier from I-10, is **Hwy. 111,** connecting at Indio. The byway services the towns of Coachella, Thermal and Mecca and leads directly to the entrance of Joshua Tree.

This desert rural route concentrates on the farming of dates and citrus fruits. Authentic Mexican restaurants can be found in Mecca, across from the train station. Try *La Conchitas* for lean carne asada tacos. If the draft Mexican beer is too tempting, find a spot to siesta.

For additional tours in the area see Anza-Borrego, Ortega Highway, and Big Bear Tours.

JOSHUA TREE HIGHLIGHTS

Approximate Mileage: 340 miles round trip from Los Angeles

Road Ratings:
FWY 60/ SLABBER; can get congested, hilly, scenic in parts.
I-10/ SLABBER; congested, trucks, possible desert winds and
   sandstorms.
JOSHUA TREE PARK ROAD/ MEANDERER; 2-lane, curves, scenic, tourists.
HWY. 62/ SLABBER; 2-lane, hilly, scenic.
HWY 111/ MEANDERER; 2 - 4 lane, good pavement.

Weather:
Hot in summer; thunderstorms rare but possible, and can flood
canyons and washes. Carry water. Dress in layers, fall through
spring.

Accommodations:
K-B Ranchotel, Twentynine Palms, adobe B&B. (760) 367-3353
Gardens Motel, Twentynine Palms, pool, spa. (760) 367-9141
29 Palms Inn, Twentynine Palm, adobe cottages, pool, restaurant.
   (760) 367-3505
Super 8 Motel, Yucca Valley, biker's discount. (760) 228-1773
Yucca Inn, Yucca Valley. (760) 365-3311
Pioneer Town Motel, Pioneer Town. (760) 365-4879

Restaurants:
Hutchins Harley-Davidson Route 62 Diner, 55405 29 Palms Hwy.,
   Yucca Valley, (760) 365-6311.
La Conchitas, Mecca, across from train station.
Pappy & Harriet's, Pioneer Town, (760) 365-5956.

Attractions:
Joshua Tree National Park   Pioneer Town

Local Harley-Davidson Dealers:
HUTCHINS HARLEY-DAVIDSON, 55405 29 Palms Hwy. Yucca Valley,
   (760) 365-6311 (and the Route 62 Diner.)
HARLEY-DAVIDSON OF VICTORVILLE, 14522 Valley Center Dr.,
   Victorville, (760) 951-1119
PALM SPRINGS HARLEY-DAVIDSON, 19465 N. Indian, North Palm
   Springs, (760) 329-1448

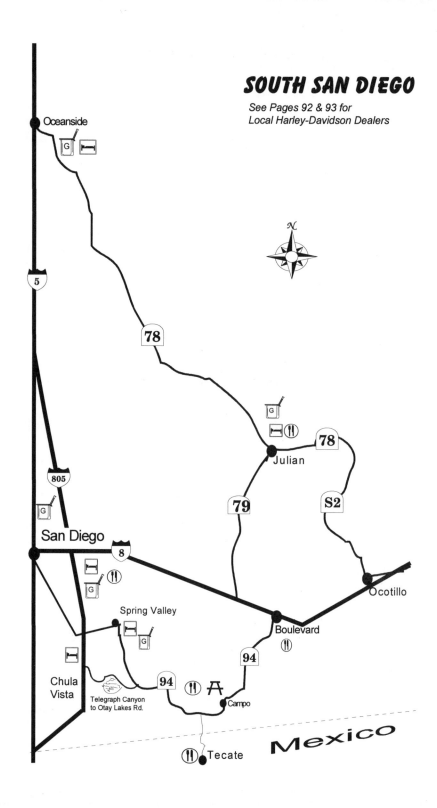

SOUTH SAN DIEGO

See Pages 92 & 93 for
Local Harley-Davidson Dealers

Oceanside

5

78

Julian

78

805

S2

79

San Diego

8

Ocotillo

Spring Valley

Boulevard

Chula Vista

94

94

Telegraph Canyon
to Otay Lakes Rd.

Campo

Tecate

Mexico

SOUTH SAN DIEGO COUNTY/ JULIAN

Although this territory looks like the stark, futuristic setting in "Mad Max" movies, it's rich with history of the wild frontier. Past, present, or future, the sparsely populated location near the border means freedom of the road to bikers. In addition to historic byways and two-bit towns, the region has plenty of riding diversity.

The journey begins on **I-805** which you can reach either by slabbing your way to San Diego or linking your favorite tours to connect with **I-5** near San Diego. There are relatively inexpensive hotels off **I-8** between I-805 and Hwy. 163 in *Hotel Circle* if you need to break up the trip. Be sure to begin the ride with a full tank of fuel as gas stops are limited.

From I-805, slabbers can exit at **Hwy. 94.** Continue on to Spring Valley where the road becomes a scenic, 2-lane,

country highway. There will be 30 miles of twisting back road that services the scattered farms and ranches.

Meanderers and benders will appreciate a more scenic run by continuing on I-805 and exiting at **L Street** onto **Telegraph Canyon Road,** to *Otay Lakes.* This route will link later to Hwy. 94. Upon exiting the freeway, the road is a 2-lane, fantastic ride and only gets better as blooming hills become rolling pastures that eventually become a landscape of sculpted boulders.

Besides excellent road conditions, the remote terrain is void of civilization. There is potential for water pockets at low points, but overall one can concentrate on sights and riding skills.

Follow Hwy. 94 east to the intersection of **Hwy. 188** (Tecate Junction). Here, you have the option to take Hwy 188 south for about a mile, and cross the border into Tecate, Mexico. As with most Baja border towns, you can spend a day making deals on silver and Kahlua, but, there is a lot more to see and do back in the States. After munching a few cheap tacos come back across the border and continue on Hwy. 94 for 12 miles to Campo, Calif.

For train buffs, The *San Diego Railroad Museum* at the Campo Depot on Forest Gate Road has a large collection of vintage trains, some which are available for riding. Tours of the equipment and restoration shops can again divert your attention from the saddle.

At the Depot, there are a variety of eating opportunities. The *Old Oak Inn* restaurant, a market, and a picnic area can provide a full lunch or a snack. Outside Campo there is the little town of *Cameron Corners,* where you can get an ice cream and a cheap haircut.

Chicken lovers might want to hold onto their appetites to get up the road 14 miles to Boulevard for raved-about broasted chicken.

Although road maps denote towns in the area with dots big enough to make you think there will be services, don't depend on it. Gas stations and restaurants open and close when they feel like it, so it's best to fill up tanks, tires and tums at any opportunity. Many towns amount to nothing more than an intersection. At the intersection in Boulevard, is where you'll find the deli for chicken or sandwiches.

At Boulevard you have the option of continuing on Hwy. 94 for another 10 miles or hopping on I-8 to Ocotillo.

The interstate freeway ride might actually be the more scenic route. It dissects the Jacumba Mountains with granite peaks and pinon pines, recently designated for protected wilderness. The area's surrealistic and stark geology is becoming a popular scene for sunset photographers. There are designated hiking trails that lead to unusual landscapes. Fortunately, much of the awesome scenery is visable from the saddle.

Jacumba Mountains will drop into the Yuha Desert, a dramatic change from the coastal mountains at the beginning of the trip. Take a left into Ocotillo for gas or refreshments before hopping on **S-2**, the old Butterfield Stage Run.

You'll be following in the tracks of the popular stage that religiously crossed over the territory between St. Louis and California during the 19th century. The Overland Mail Co., a postal run of the Butterfield Stage Co. was known for its expeditious, 28-day delivery time. The route had to migrate north to the Oregon Trail during the Civil

War.

On S-2 you'll cross Earthquake Valley (though locals with real estate call it Shelter Valley). A 50-mile underground fault zone with more unusual rock formations and a crumbling crust, create badlands to admire. If you ride in spring, the stark surroundings are softened by bouquets of wildflowers and blooming ocotillo.

You'll think that portions of this desert road were engineered by a biker. The sweeping curves and general layout are not the typical stretches associated with desert riding. Occasionally, you'll hit stretches that will tease you into saddle sleep, but then desert passes with hairpin curves will arise and break up any riding monotony.

The road has one last climb to Hwy. 78 and a stretch begins that will demand perpetual right hand twists into downward motion. To make this stretch appear even more repetitive, similar looking curves pass a stream in the same position off the road. You are moving in a forwardly direction, however, and in about 18 miles the junction to Julian will break the vehicular trance. Take a left onto **Hwy 78**.

A historic goldmining town, *Julian* is now surrounded by fruit orchards. The popular tourist town, best known for its apples, markets everything that could contain or bear the fruit. If you're not loaded down with goods from Mexico and have a couple of bungee cords, strap a pie on the back of your bike to take home.

Along with apples, Julian is flavored by a western past. Rustic storefronts house specialty shops stocked with country crafts and gifts. Cafes serving apple pie and coffee are located in every block. There's also a museum and original jail cell in the heart of town.

If pie and coffee don't rev you up for the ride home, you can check into one of the local inns for a good night's rest. There are old historic lodgings in the heart of town or rustic and remote cabins in the surrounding hills. Spend the weekend with a loved one or a good book. The Julian Chamber of Commerce listed in the Highlights and Tourist Information Sections assist with reservations throughout the area.

Many roads lead out of Julian and which one to take depends on your mood and timetable. **Hwy. 79** will take you back to San Diego, **Hwy. 78** to Oceanside, and **Highways**

74, **15**, and **91** will zip you back into the Los Angeles area.

Alternate roads for benders are **S1** from Julian to I-8 or Hwy. 94, a fun and twisty road up Laguna Mountain that connects to Hwy. 79. It's also another way to tour South San Diego toward Julian.

Heading north from Julian, an alternate way back into the Los Angeles area is Mesa Grande Road that connects to Hwy. 79 near Santa Ysabel. The scenic, 12-mile route skirts the Mesa Grande Indian Reservation and many mines. The road connects to **Hwy. 76** near Lake Henshaw to continue back toward Riverside and other counties.

You can easily connect with other tours from most of these back roads. See Anza-Borrego, Ortega Highway/ San Jacinto, Joshua Tree, and Pacific Coast Highway South Tours.

For those who are confident with their riding skills, (for example, being able to swerve around cattle and potholes), touring Baja California is liberating and ruggedly scenic. However, no matter your skill level, the desolate inland regions are not recommended during hot weather.

From Tecate, taking Mexican **Hwy. 2**, east, cuts through the Rumorosa Grade, an exhilarating run with a terrain of sheer drops and cliff walls. At the bottom of the grade, you can treasure hunt for opals.

You can re-enter California at Calexico, just north of Mexicali, (about 80 miles from Tecate on Hwy. 2) and jump on I-8, or continue on backroads to link up with other tours.

Mexican Hwy. 2, west, from Tecate leads to Tijuana (about 35 miles) and **Trans-peninsular Highway 1,** the coast run south to Ensenada and other popular vacation areas. There are actually two highways, the free (*libre*) road and the toll road (Hwy. 1D). For longer treks (beyond Rosarito), the scenic and winding free route provides entertaining curves and superb coastal views.

It's not uncommon for gas stations to run out of fuel. Be sure to carry a map and plan alternate fuel stops. For more information on touring across the border, check with your local touring group or contact a southern San Diego dealer.

SOUTHERN SAN DIEGO/ JULIAN HIGHLIGHTS

Approximate Mileage: 385 miles round trip from Los Angeles

Road Ratings:
I-5/ SLABBER; multi-lane freeway with heavy traffic.
I-805/ SLABBER; multi-lane freeway with average traffic.
HWY. 94/ MEANDERER; 2-lane, scenic, twists and turns.
I-8/ SLABBER; multi-lane freeway with light traffic, scenic, hills.
S-2/ MEANDERER; 2-lane, historic pass, straightaways, curves.
HWY. 78/ MEANDERER; 2-lane, scenic, winding, country road.
HWY. 79/ MEANDERER; 2-lane, scenic, winding, mountainous.

Weather:
Warm to hot in summer, pleasant in spring and fall. Can get cold in winter. Julian area is generally cooler than desert.

Restaurants:
Old Oak Inn, Campo Depot
Boulevard Deli, Boulevard
Julian Cafe, Main & B Streets
Julian Grille, Main & Washington Streets
Mom's Pies, Main & B Streets

Accommodations:
Roadway Inn, La Mesa, enroute, inexpensive. (619) 589-7288
Howard Johnson, Hotel Circle, spa, coffeeshop. 800-446-4656
Julian Lodge, historic inn located in town. (760) 765-1420
Pine Hills Lodge, outside Julian, restaurant. (760) 765-1100

Attractions:
Tecate, Mexico	San Diego Railroad Museum
Campo	Jacumba Mountains & Wilderness Park
Julian	

Local Harley-Davidson Dealers:
HARLEY-DAVIDSON OF EL CAJON, 621 El Cajon Blvd., El Cajon,
     (619) 444-1123
SOUTH COAST HARLEY-DAVIDSON, 345 E Street, San Diego, Chula Vista,
     (619) 420-7000

SAN MARCOS PASS/ SANTA MARIA

See Pages 92 & 93 for Local Harley-Davidson Dealers

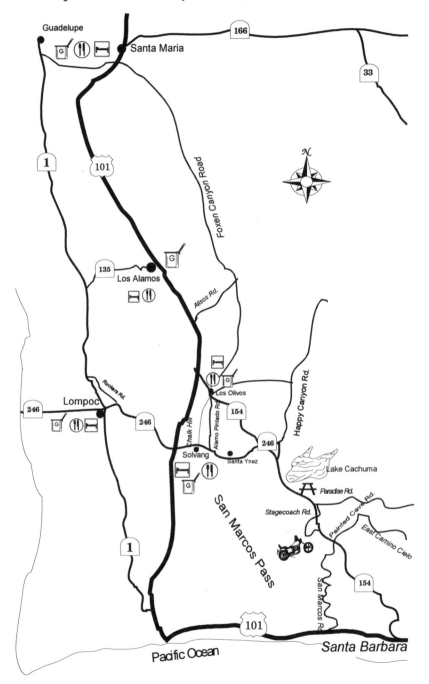

Strap a 10-gallon hat over your helmet and take a ride into the old West via the **San Marcos Pass**. California's last stage ran through this territory, leaving riding trails of all levels to enjoy. The only modernization on many of these back roads, originally blazed to thwart bandits lusting over the Wells Fargo strong box, is the addition of pavement and power lines.

There is more riding opportunity around the pass than described on this tour. However, some of the roads have steep gravel sections or lead out of the pass quickly. If you'd like to explore more routes in the area, purchase a Santa Barbara County map which will provide the detail needed on the remote back roads.

To reach the area, hop on **Hwy. 101** to Santa Barbara. (Or take the Pacific Coast Highway Tour, Mullholland Tour, or the the Ojai Tour.) From Hwy. 101 exit on **San Marcos Pass, Hwy. 154,** the 30-mile scenic route through the Santa Ynez Valley. The road is two lanes until the crest and then it widens into a four lane highway.

On the ascent into the region, every curve contains breathtaking views of Santa Barbara, Goleta, and the Channel Islands. You'll want eyes in the back of your head to enjoy the bird's eye view of the coast, but don't gawk too long because chances are you're gaining on the butt of a motor home. Use vista points for soaking up the sights.

Don't be surprised if motorists are also gawking at you. There is a lot of curiosity from non-riders in this area.

For benders, the most challenging route onto the Pass is isolated **San Marcos Road**, off the Turnpike exit from Hwy. 101, a few miles north of the Hwy. 154 turnoff. Although this narrow road is strikingly panoramic, you won't have much chance to enjoy the view as you conquer corkscrew turns up steep grades on cliffs without guard rails. This route was an old favorite of bandits. Hair pin turns made stage holdups a sit down job. You'll wonder how in the hell a bulky ash-and-oak coach with horses managed.

San Marcos Road intersects with San Marcos Pass about 3 miles up near **Painted Cave Road**, which begins across the Pass. One of the state's rare archeological sites is located about a mile up, a Chumash cave painting. Through these visual messages, the tribe told wandering groups about local weather, food, and water conditions.

The road is a pretty, concrete trail with homes tucked into naturally landscaped surroundings. Keeping to the left, Painted Cave merges with roads leading back to the Pass. Turning right on **East Camino Cielo** will take you through Rattlesnake Canyon and back down to Montecito near the botanical gardens. Portions of this road are designated as gravel and dirt, and probably should only be considered by the truly adventurous or masochistic.

Paradise Road which leads to several campgrounds can also have gravelly sections until it dead ends into a picnic area. A river periodically chases this 8-mile trek.

The most popular scooter route is **Stagecoach Road,** intersecting the Pass at the crest. You'll want to make a left across the highway, keeping in mind that opposing traffic can be travelling as fast as on a freeway.

After turning onto Stagecoach Road, you'll want to bear to the right when the roads splits. You'll weave through a woodsy setting, and then drop down into even a more picturesque area. Around the bend and nestled to one side of a stream is *Cold Springs Tavern.*

Once a stage stop, the rustic, 125-year old building is now a biker hangout, especially popular on Sundays. Live music, a fire and laughter radiates inside. You'll think that your boots have sprouted spurs as you bite into a buffalo or venison sandwich.

If you want to remain outdoors, head to the patio where a **BBQ** chef will be cooking up a tri-tip roast. The cabins behind the patio have housed many legal and illegal activities since the 19th century, including a Chinese worker railroad camp.

Stagecoach Road will loop back to Hwy. 154. Set the throttle at 35 mph and enjoy the brief freedom ride on this peaceful route, leaving bungee jumping civilization at the sweeping bridge behind you.

Once back on Hwy. 154, you'll undoubtedly join RV's and tourists. Settle back and enjoy the road's roller coaster effect, Lake Cachuma, and the rambling hills spattered with lazy oaks. There is little opportunity for passing, and be aware that police patrol regularly. Relief comes shortly ahead.

When Hwy. 154 intersects with **Hwy. 246**, you'll find most vehicles heading toward Solvang, and the highway will open up. However, by continuing on, you'll miss the western town of Santa Ynez, located just off Hwy. 246 before Solvang.

In Santa Ynez you can stretch road legs on wooden sidewalks and watch ranchers in cowboy hats fetch their mail in the century-old post office. Don't miss the old outhouse near the real estate office. *Mission of Santa Inez* is also nearby. Gas is available in both Santa Ynez and Solvang.

Sightseeing is a must in the popular Danish village of Solvang if you're a chocoholic or in need of a cuckoo clock. Even the area's most notorious bandit, Salomon Pico, probably wouldn't have passed up a gooey hot cross bun and cup of coffee if the Danish had

migrated a little earlier. Hwy. 246 will meet up with Hwy. 101 at Buelton where you can find inexpensive, no-frills lodging and a bowl of famous Andersen pea soup.

If you continue on Hwy. 154 or get back on the Pass by taking **Alamo Pintado Road** from Hwy. 246 you'll reach the town of Los Olivos and *Mattei's Tavern* at the junction. The original stage stop and restaurant is still catering to whiskey-and-beer-chasing riders, or those who'd like to admire the long bar and historic photo collection with a Sasparilla. You can also eat on an outdoor patio or take a snack out to a bench in the rose garden.

The town of Los Olivos caters to the wine tasting and gallery browsing crowd. Here, you'll find ritzy bed & breakfast retreats with Jacuzzi and tea time. Don't work on your bike in front of the lobby if you intend to join the other guests with an evening glass of sherry. A small gas stop is in the heart of town, but don't expect a leather-clad group to be milling around it, either, in this quiet community.

Hwy. 154 connects to Hwy. 101 three-miles north of Los Olivos. Santa Maria is just another 20 miles through the rolling hills on open highway.

If you're not ready for super slabbing, try taking **Foxen Canyon Road,** a scenic putt through the hills, which joins the Pass across from Mattei's Tavern.

Foxen Canyon Road is an undivided road that leads to wineries—watch for "just-say-yes" tipsy tasters. The gravelly, old pavement also encourages a putt rather than speed drive.

Along the way, you'll periodically encounter a shady canopy of oak trees and possibly light aircraft. Locals borrow the road to land their small Cessnas, the preferred mode of transportation for long commutes. You can chat with neighbors while the plane gets parked. This alternative route plops you in the heart of Santa Maria in about the same amount time as taking Hwy. 101. Foxen Canyon Road turns into **Betteravia Road** in Santa Maria.

If you're ready to call it a day, the refurbished *Santa Maria Inn* offers the nicest bed and amenities in the area. There's a Jacuzzi, pool, restaurant and bar, all on the premises. You won't have to get in the saddle until morning when you might want to take **Main Street** to **Hwy. 1** toward Guadalupe, about 10 miles away. Look for an old brick building with a cloud of smoke. *Far Western Tavern* should be barbequing up lunch by late morning.

Benders still lusting after more road can take **Hwy. 166** East. You'll cruise over hill and dale, passing the Twitchell Reservoir. The ride is not straightaway fast, but not hairpin slow, as long as you don't get stuck behind a local hay truck. Hwy. 166 leads to Bakersfield where you'll find Basque dining and more riding opportunity. (See Kern County/ Sherman Pass Tour.)

If you prefer to soak up the Old West ambiance around San Marcos Pass, you can also soak your feet just 10 miles up the road off Hwy. 101 in the "Den of Thieves," or **Los Alamos**. Once the hideout of stage bandits, the town today displays no indication of city tax expenditures since the invention of the lamp post, and the townsfolk are proud of it. On the main drag is the *Los Alamos Bed and Breakfast*, a renovated Western lodging house complete with footed bath tubs and some rooms with Murphy beds.

After a family-style dinner, everyone heads into the saloon for more banter and booze, just like Salomon Pico enjoyed after a robbery, adorned with his necklace of gringo ears. He liked to dump the rest of his victim behind the town in Skull Canyon- ask for directions.

From Los Alamos you can link up to scenic rural back roads into Lompoc. (Also from Santa Maria via Hwy. 1.) **Hwy. 135**, a pastoral and remote route meanders peacefully with enough curves and dips to keep your riding interest while watching grazing animals and gliding birds of prey.

One of California's most authentic missions, the *La Purisma de Concepcion* is a sightseeing stop along the journey. Turn off Hwy. 135 at Harris Grade (also Old Hwy. 1) and continue south-west 5 miles to **Ruckers Road**. The mission is at the junction with Hwy. 246. Horses still graze in the field and cowhides tan on the racks. Hacienda-style buildings display all facets of mission culture. You can picnic on the grassy field if you plan ahead and bring lunch.

Hwy. 246 west will continue on to Lompoc where you'll find an unrushed, Midwestern spirited community. There are several places for fuel and food in the heart of the town.

Don't be fooled by the sparkling sun in this region. Usually it's accompanied by brisk ocean air swooping over those rolling hills and even in June you want to dress in layers and bring warm gloves.

Lompoc is considered the flower seed capital. If you have hay fever, one good inhale of fresh air might have you sneezing the rest of your life. Don't forget the antihistimines if you're a sinus sufferer. However annoying the pollens might be, the patchquilt of blooming colors is worth seeing and is at a peak from late April through June.

There are a variety of good roads to explore in the area. The tourist information center provides maps of the area and directions to look out points where you can ride by the gardens and get descriptions on what's growing. Benders can spend an entire day zigzagging across the valley from Hwy. 1 to Hwy. 101.

You can continue from Lompoc to the central coast, a pristine area so isolated you might only encounter some sheep and a surfer searching for the perfect wave. Journey out to Vandenburg Air Force Base and you might get to see a missle being fired up, always a spectacular sight.

When you can't put it off any longer, and you have to think homeward bound, take Hwy. 1 south back to Hwy. 101. Santa Barbara, Carpinteria, or Ventura provide a pleasant pit stop from the road pounding and have gas and snacks just off the freeway.

Santa Maria-bound super slabbers will find just as much delight in bypassing the Pass and staying on Hwy. 101. Once beyond the San Fernando Valley, the route is pleasant and diverse. You'll weave down to Camarillo and meet the sea in Ventura. Once outside Santa Barbara, hawks will be waiting to glide with you. Rolling hills, eucalyptus trees and a clacking train are just some of the scenes along the old Camino Real.

When Hwy. 101 curves due north at Gaviota State Park stay clear of wobbly motor homes and tour buses. Gusty winds in the region might take you by surprise. Towns become more remote in this area. A good gas opportunity is located at Buellton where you can also warm up with a bowl of split-pea soup at famous Andersen's restaurant.

SAN MARCOS PASS/ SANTA MARIA HIGHLIGHTS

Approximate Mileage: 360 miles round trip from Los Angeles

Road Ratings:
HWY 101/ SLABBER; multi-lane, scenic climbing and winding.
SAN MARCOS PASS/ (HWY. 154)/ SLABBER; scenic, 2 - 4 lane
     highway, climbing, winding, usually congested with RVs.
SAN MARCOS ROAD/ BENDER; 2-lane unmarked, corkscrew turns,
     steep, ridge road, views.
STAGECOACH ROAD/ MEANDERER; 1- & 2- lane, scenic, winding.
PARADISE OR PAINTED CAVE ROADS/ MEANDERER; 2-lane unmarked,
     scenic, winding, gravelly sections.
HWY. 1/ BENDER; 2-lane, level, pastoral.
FOXEN CANYON/ MEANDERER; 2-lane, unmarked, winding, scenic, wineries.

Weather:
Usually 5- to 10-degrees warmer than coastal temperatures and can
become windy. Nights are cool. Dress in layers.

Restaurants:
Cold Springs Tavern, 5995 Stagecoach Rd. (805) 967-0066
Mattei's Tavern, Hwy. 154 Junction, Los Olivos. (805) 688-4820
Far Western Tavern, 899 Guadalupe St., Guadalupe. (805) 343-2211
Solvang
Andersen's Split Pea, Buellton. 800-PEASOUP.

Overnight Accommodations:
Los Alamos Union Hotel, 362 Bell Street, Los Alamos.
     (805) 344-2744
Los Olivos Grand Hotel, 2860 Grand Ave., Los Olivos. 800-446-2455
Andersen's Inn, 51E. Hwy. 246, Buellton. 800-PEASOUP
Santa Maria Inn, 801 S. Broadway, Santa Maria. (805) 928-7777

Attractions:
Wineries	Santa Ynez	Solvang
Painted Cave	Missions	

Local Harley-Davidson Dealer:
HARLEY-DAVIDSON OF SANTA MARIA, 601 W. Main St., Santa Maria,
     (805) 928-3668
VENTURA HARLEY-DAVIDSON, 1326 Del Norte Blvd., Camarillo,
     (805) 981-9904

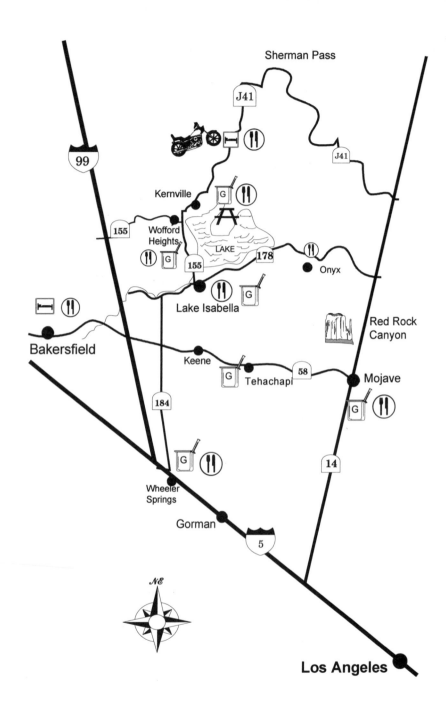

Sherman Pass

J41

99

J41

Kernville

G

155

Wofford
Heights

LAKE

155

178

Onyx

Lake Isabella

G

Bakersfield

Keene

G   Tehachapi

58

Red Rock
Canyon

Mojave

G

184

G

Wheeler
Springs

14

Gorman

5

Nℰ

Los Angeles

KERN RIVER/ SHERMAN PASS

See Pages 92 & 93 for Local Harley-Davidson Dealers

When you wake up with your foot in a kickstart spasm, ready to ride the world all at once, where can you go? Here's a tour that can't be beat for riding terrain and scenic pleasure. You can twist and turn along rivers and lakes, climb mountains like a motorgoat, and break loose on isolated straightaways.

Pop a wheelie out of your driveway and head north through the Angeles Forest to Lake Isabella and Sherman Pass (Sherman Pass is closed in winter).

This all-day, "big-dog" run starts on **Hwy. 2** through the Angeles Forest, links up with **N3** toward Palmdale, from which you either remain on **Sierra Highway** or hop on

Hwy. 14 to Mojave.

You'll ride through the Santa Clarita Valley and past Edwards Air Force Base. The landscape will convert to open desert and there won't be much more than road and shrubs until the town of Mojave.

Hwy. 14 becomes a commercial stretch with a line of gas stations, coffee shops, and fast food restaurants. Left over from the '50s are roadside motels and coffee shops if you need a cup or breakfast.

Continuing on Hwy. 14, in about 40 miles, you'll come to Red Rock Canyon, a region of multicolored sandstone cliffs naturally carved by time into wonderful shapes. You might see an occasional eagle or coyote in the area. Hwy. 14 cuts through the scenic park that has camping and picnicking.

At **Hwy. 178** head west to Lake Isabella. The road enters Walkers Pass, an ascent into a forest of Joshua Trees and descent into a valley with open stretches, panoramic views, and usually no RVs.

The town of Onyx has one of the oldest operating markets in the state. Grab a drink to quench your thrist from the desert dust and check out the decor.

Back on your bike and continuing toward the lake, you might witness the new growth from recent fires. Sweeping curves follow the form of the Kern River, and big boulders line the road through this lower end of the Sequoias. Unlike its raging counterpart on the other side of the lake, the Kern River in this section is a peaceful companion to tranquil, grassy surroundings complete with grazing cattle.

Arriving at Lake Isabella, a man-made dam for the Kern River, there will be several lakeside villages for food and gas. A cafe called the *Dam Korner* Store in the main town of Lake Isabella has damn good food!

Following the rim of Lake Isabella by bearing right onto **Hwy. 155**, you will reach the north end and resort towns of Wofford Heights and Kernville. Wofford Heights is less crowded than Kernville and considered a more swank area to dine and stroll. Food and gas are also available in the more casual Kernville, a perfect spot for picking up a sandwich and picnicking along the lakeside park. The lake as well as river area is crowded with recreational users so ride defensively.

A tucked away lodge which might be more intriguing to bikers is on the highway out of Kernville, about 10 miles up. It's called *Johnny McNallys* and grills steaks worth waiting for. Both food and service is good enough to keep you overnight. For those who are determined to make it to Sherman Pass, continue on about 10 more miles to reach a town called "Road Ends," but don't take that literally. Make a right into the community and ride to **J-41** which starts the serious climb to Sherman Pass. (As the road is closed in winter, check with the Highway Patrol if you are thinking about riding near snow season. The number is listed in the highlights section.) The pass isn't death defying, but is challenging with a twisting, contorted climb to 9200 feet that could wear out novice riders.

After an Alpine climb through the pines to the top, stop at the lookout point. There is a description of all the mountain ranges in view, including Mt. Whitney, the state's highest peak. Spend enough time to undizzy yourself, because the way down is a 50-mile descent onto the desert floor. You'll make good time on the mountain curves and shortly be in the Mojave Desert again.

At Pearsonville you can gas up or grab a bite to recharge for the ride home. Hop on **Hwy. 14** and head south, hoping someone is willing to give you a massage after a hot bath at your destination.

An alternate route off Hwy. 14, either coming or going, is **Hwy. 58** which runs through the hilly Tehachapi Valley from Hwy. 14 to Bakersfield. There is still wildlife in the area and it's possible to spot an eagle or condor circling in and out of the hills.

Along the way you'll pass through the towns of Tehachapi and Keene, where you can see the famous Tehachapi train loop. T h e engineering marvel allowed train travel through the mountain range and was the main vein to Bakersfield's farming and oil development. Arriving at the right time, you can see a freighter circle like a snake through the pass. Another attraction in Keene is the 100-year-old post office. There are signs to direct you to both points of interest.

An off-the-beaten-pavement side route in this area is **Oak Creek Pass** which you can take outside Tehachapi and link up again with Hwy. 14.

If a big dog run to Sherman Pass sounds more exhausting than exhilerating, a far less macho ride is continuing on **Hwy. 155** at Wofford Heights at the lake. This little side putt is a pleasant run down the mountain and into the fertile valley north of Bakersfield. You can hop on either **Hwy. 65** or **Hwy. 99** south toward Bakersfield.

By remaining on Hwy. 178 and following the Kern River, you will also drop down to Bakersfield and enjoy another kind of scenic ride. The tranquil setting experienced before the lake is whisked away by the south fork of the Kern River, a tributary for Mt. Whitney's run off. Its unforgiving rapids rip through boulders and is the popular rafting run.

The valley will start to squeeze into the mouth of a canyon. Through this natural chute, the Kern gradually becomes more wild and river rafters will surface. You can pull off and watch a group get air off a rapid and think about exchanging your leather vest one weekend for a Mae West. Phone numbers of tours are in the towns along the lake.

Hwy. 178 will drop down into Bakersfield where you can spend the night to rest up for another day of riding or take a break before hitting the freeway.

The town's tourist claim to fame is Basque dining, a multicourse meal with such delights as pickled tongue. At *Pyrennes,* one of the original peasant restaurants, you'll be served in the traditional family style at benches behind the bar room. (If someone smells like a sheep next to you, there are a few shepherds left in the area.) There are more touristy Basque places along the main stretch into town.

You can bypass Bakersfield by turning off Hwy. 178 about 30 miles from the Lake at **Hwy. 184**, a farm road that parallels Hwy. 99, taking you to Wheeler Ridge and the **I-5**. On hot summer days, on the south side of the freeway exit you can cool down with the radiator water hose.

Over the Grapevine, through Santa Clarita Valley and into Los Angeles basin you'll go. Although I-5 gets a bad rap for being boring, it's actually a nice ending to a full day. It's about the only place left with a vast expanse of land underneath folding hills that resemble tanned leather. You'll climb the Grapevine, pass Pyramid and Castaic Lakes and the amusement rides confined to Magic Mountain. If the day is still young there are exits for exploring the state's travel backbone.

At Lebec you'll see signs for *Fort Tejon,* a restored army fort and famous for its living history programs such as the Civil War re-enactments. The fort is open for tours where you can learn more about local and significant State history. Call (805) 248-6692 for hours.

You can witness truck culture at the *Truck Stop America* exit just before the Grapevine. Steal a pet name for your bike off the side of a Peterbilt in the parked sea of triple axles. Inside the complex, there are different restaurants and a truck store where you can admire all the mud flaps and hemorrhoid medicines that America makes.

From Hwy. 14 and I-5 you can link up with the Ojai, Angeles Forest, or Death Valley Tours.

KERN COUNTY/ SHERMAN PASS HIGHLIGHTS

Approximate Mileage: 450 miles round trip from Los Angeles

Road Ratings:
I-5/ SLABBER; multi-lane straightaway with Grapevine hill.
HWY. 184/ MEANDERER; straightaway, 2-lane farm road.
HWY. 178/ MEANDERER; 2-lane, scenic, curves, valley and river runs.
J-41/ BENDER; unmarked, scenic, climbs from 2,500 - 9,200 ft.
HWY 14/ SLABBER; multi-lane desert straigthaway.
HWY. 58/ MEANDERER; 2-lane, hilly chaparral, scenic.
HWY. 99/ SLABBER; multi-lane, straightaway, some traffic.

Weather:
Sherman Pass closed in winter. Call CHP, (800) 427-7623, for road conditions. Pass can be cool year round with thunder storms. Desert has weather extremes, hot in summer, cold in winter, with winds near Mojave. Wear layers to ride from mountain to desert conditions.

Restaurants:
Dam Korner, 6303 Lake Isabella Blvd., Lake Isabella,
        (760) 379-8770.
Johnny McNalley's, Mountain 99, Fairview. (760) 376-2430.
Pyrenee's, 601 Sumner, Bakersfield. (661) 323-0053

Attractions:
Red Rock Canyon
Kern River
Lake Isabella
Sherman Pass View Area
Tehachapi Train Loop
Keene Post Office
Fort Tejon

Local Harley-Davidson Dealers:
THORP'S HARLEY-DAVIDSON, INC., 820 - 824 18th Street, Bakersfield,
        (661) 325-3644
HARLEY-DAVIDSON OF LANCASTER, 45313 23rd St., Lancaster,
        (661) 948-5959

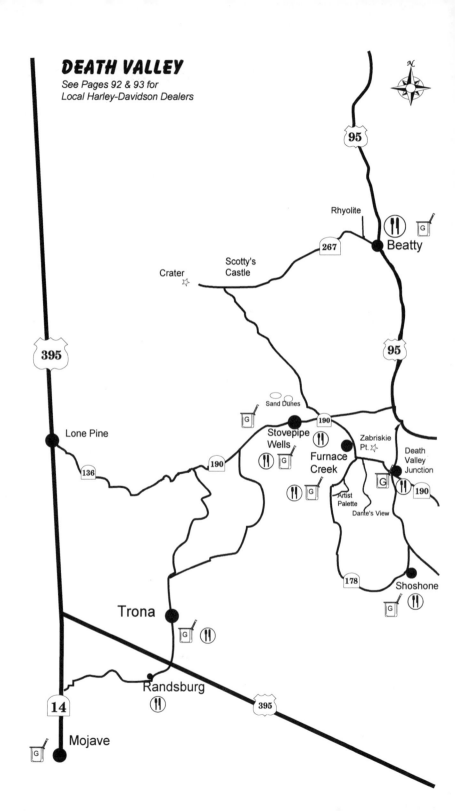

DEATH VALLEY

Excellent roads and world-renown scenery make Death Valley a strong calling card. However, it is one of the hottest places on earth in the summer. Plan a trip in spring or fall. Temperatures in general are pleasant in the winter, but the higher elevations are blistering cold.

Several routes will lead to **Hwy. 14** and put you on your way. In addition to **I-5** which connects to Hwy. 14 in Canyon Country, **Hwy. 2** to **I-210** to I-5 offers a little more scenery along the foothills and is often a lot less travelled.

N3 (described in the Canyon Country Tour) from Hwy. 2 cuts through the Angeles Forest and links up to Hwy. 14, too. A good or experienced rider can probably travel through the mountains in the same amount of time as taking the slabber routes. By taking Hwy. 14 to the San Fernando exit, and 5 miles to Saugus, you'll find the Saugus Cafe for a country breakfast with a homey atmosphere.

Hwy. 14 is known for its wind tunnels as it cuts through the canyon. Once you've made it through to the desert floor these conditions often subside. Riding through Palmdale and Lancaster, it's more scenic to look in the rear view mirror at the Angeles Forest, but soon you'll pass your last Osco and Von's and leave civilization as you know it.

Mojave is the first of two-bit desert towns and the gateway into desert culture. The towns get more interesting as you climb into the high desert on well maintained, 2-lane roads. There's plenty of places to gas up along the commercial stretch in Mojave before continuing north on Hwy. 14 toward Garlock.

On this journey with long stretches of isolation, it's wise to fill up whenever you see a fuel pump, particularly peanut tanks. On smaller bikes, consider carrying extra gas. A little wind and unexpected ascent might be the determining factor of running out a mile or two short. Gas stations are located at Jawbone Junction and Trona. After Trona, there's not a drop until Stovepipe Wells, about 80 miles.

Jawbone Junction primarily serves the dirt bike crowd. There is a misting garden where bikers go to cool down and rinse off grime. On a hot day, it's a welcome stop for anyone exposed to the heat to mist off and pull a cool drink from the market's fridge.

Continue on Hwy. 14 until the junction with directions to Garlock or Randsburg/ Red Mountain. Choose Randsburg/ Red Mountain. Either way will lead to Trona-Wildrose Highway and Death Valley, but the Randsburg direction is through old Gold Rush territory.

Randsburg should technically be a ghost town but enough interested people have kept it alive and authentic. Have lunch at the White House Saloon, where the pickled eggs are worth the indigestion. There's even one room for rent in town if you need to lie down, complete with a claw foot tub and desert views.

The highway intersects with Hwy. 395 by Red Mountain, cross it to continue on toward Johannesburg (these towns were named for the lucky mining areas of South Africa).

Instead of trying to remember names or highway numbers here, just remember you want to see red— that's the color of the asphalt to Trona. You'll be glad to know that your eyes aren't sun damaged. It's an excellent road over the hills. Descending into the valley, you'll arrive in the contemporary mining town. Do remember, it's last call for gas until Death Valley.

Trona is a town unto its own as workers buzz around the putrid smelling trona mine. It's an interesting stop that can also provide a meal, the last until Stovepipe Wells. If you're travelling late, you should probably fill up on food and fuel.

The *Yacht Club* on the east side of the highway on the southern end of town is a friendly stop with a funky saloon. For a faster bite, there's the Tornado Sandwich Shop or Last Chance Pizza Place also on the strip.

From Trona, continue on **Trona Wildrose Road.** Over each pass on the 2-lane highway, you'll anticipate park boundaries. Winter weather conditions make for a rough ride year round on the last five mile stretch, just before **Hwy. 190**. To avoid this section, take a left at Panamint Valley Road and then a right at Hwy. 190 to Stovepipe Wells.

Panamint Mountains and Valley will be the last tease before park boundaries. Panamint's peaks are composed of Earth's oldest rocks, submerged under the sea 200 million years ago and embedded with the fossils of many marine mammals.

At the pass when you look down, you'll know you've arrived at Death Valley by the striking sand dunes that look as if UFO's have left their imprint on the land. You won't want to stop on the summit for long because of the contrast in temperature at the 5,000-ft. elevation, but that's OK, because there's a lot of riding ahead.

Riding Death Valley is fun because the roads are naturally carved out from the terrain. You can feel the naturalness of the turns and climbs, like a bobsled run down a mountain.

Stovepipe Wells is the first oasis for gas, food, lodging, and camping. Get a map of the area if you don't already have one to pinpoint areas of visiting interest.

The sand dunes seen coming in are near here and are a main attraction. These ever shifting mounds are spectacular, particularly when flowers are blooming on their white surfaces. Many people come in the night to see nocturnal critters scurrying over the contrasting terrain.

Most of the park's attractions are centered off of **Hwy. 190** and **Hwy. 178** (Badwater Road.) *Dante's View,* off Hwy. 190, is at the end of a smooth but slow going narrow road that climbs to a view of Death Valley's unique rock garden. Another postcard-perfect ride is off Badwater Road, *Artist Palette* loop. You'll ride through a natural gallery show of how mother nature uses rusts, lavenders, mustards, and green hues in striated beauty. It's a one-way, 1-lane curving run where you have to watch the concrete below and bumper ahead as well as the sights.

Furnace Creek is the other oasis in the park and you can sample many treats from the date palms that also provide welcome shade. There are more resort hotels here than at Stovepipe Wells. It's wise to make reservations ahead of time if you want to be assured of accommodations. Campsites are plentiful, but they fill up, too.

In the northern end of the park, there are two more attractions, *Scotty's Castle* and *Ubehebe Crater* that are both intriguing spectacles on the ominous landscape. The road up here in this remote end of the park is a little more rugged but is also fun with rollercoaster ripples. It can get a little windy on the way out to the crater.

In this neck of the rocks, there are also some graded dirt roads that might be of interest to benders or the more envigorated rider. Racetrack Valley Road by Ubehebe Crater is a popular ride and carries the lore of having rocks that leave visible tracks.

If you've had enough sights by the time you get to Scotty's Castle off **Hwy. 267**, run like a wild mustang east toward Beatty in Nevada. Only an unlucky encounter with the police can stop you on this open road that climbs out of Death Valley and crosses state lines onto a mesa of casinos.

Near Beatty off **Hwy. 374,** which will lead back into Death Valley near Stovepipe Wells, is the ruins of *Ryholite*. It's worth the side trip to see the remains of Nevada's first bustling city that almost became the capitol. Artist sculptures and in an intact bottle house are visual entertainment as you ride into the exposed grave of a boom town.

Hwy. 95 from Beatty will run you down the back side of Death Valley and by taking **Hwy. 373** to Death Valley Junction, gas up, and you can re-enter the park on Hwy. 190. A better route is continuing on California **Hwy. 127** (Nevada Hwy. 373) to Shoshone.

The desert town of Shoshone is a fun place to stretch in this lonely territory. The Red Buggy and Crowbar Saloon is an appetizing eatery and watering hole where the bar stools are old tractor seats. Ask the bartender what the letters stand for that are displayed underneath the crowbar.

The best part of taking this route through Shoshone is turning onto Hwy. 178. In Jubilee Pass you'll ride smile-filled miles back into the park. This route is a blast as you enjoy the park's scenic beauty on a road carved from the terrain and has a natural, exhilarating flow. This route will take you to the lowest elevation in the western hemisphere and link back to Hwy. 190. There's no need to see all of Death Valley in one trip, because you'll surely return the next chance you get.

Devout slabbers who reside in the southern counties can get to Death Valley by hopping on **I-15** toward Las Vegas and exiting onto **Hwy. 127**, north, at Baker. Meanderers can take I-15 to **Hwy. 58**, northwest, to **Hwy. 395**, north, to Randsburg. Either route passes through barren desert—carry water!

DEATH VALLEY HIGHLIGHTS

Approximate Mileage: 600-plus miles round trip

Road Ratings:
HWY. 14/ SLABBER; multi-lane freeway, can get windy in passes.
TRONA WILDROSE ROAD/ SLABBER; 2-lane, many passes, scenic.
HWY 190/ SLABBER; 2-lane, scenic, well-maintained, tourists.
HWY. 178/ MEANDERER; 2-lane, scenic, well-maintained, tourists.
HWY. 267/ MEANDERER; 2-lane, isolated, curves, straightaways.
HWY. 95/ BENDER; multi-lane, straightaway.
HWY. 373 & 127/ BENDER; 2-lane, straightaway.
RACETRACK/ BENDER; dirt, check conditions with local rangers.

Weather Conditions:
Dress in layers for altitude changes in spring, winter and fall.
Summer temperatures are over 120 degrees and winter is a pleasant
70 degrees but cold at higher elevations and in the night.   Carry
water and peanut tanks should carry extra gas.

Restaurants:
Saugus Cafe, San Fernando Rd. exit off Hwy. 14, then 5 miles to Saugus
White House Salon, Butte Ave., Randsburg
Red Buggy Cafe & Crowbar, Hwy. 127, Shoshone. (760) 852-9908

Accommodations:
Furnace Creek Inn, spendy with all amenities. (760) 786-2345
Furnance Creek Ranch, posh resort. (760) 786-2345
Stovepipe Wells Village, pool, store, restaurant. (760) 786-2387
Desert Rose Motel, Trona. (760) 372-4115.

Attractions:
Randsburg   Death Valley Sights
Rhyolite   Beatty

Los Angeles Harley-Davidson Dealers:
HARLEY-DAVIDSON OF LANCASTER, 45313 23rd St., Lancaster
    (661) 948-5959

MOTORCYCLE HOT SPOTS

Big Oak— 33101 Bouquet Canyon Rd., Saugus, (805) 296-5656.
See Canyon Country, page 23.
Camp Scheideck— off Lockwood Valley Road, near Hwy. 33 junction,
(805) 649-9738. *See Santa Paula/ Lockwood Valley, page 29.*
Chad's Place— 4740 Village Dr., Big Bear Lake, (909) 866-2161.
See Angeles Forest/ Big Bear, page 41.
Cold Springs Tavern— 5995 Stagecoach Rd., Santa Barbara,
(805) 967-0066. *See San Marcos Pass, page 71.*
Cook's Corner— Santiago Road & Live Oak Canyon, Trabuco.
(949) 858-0266 *See Pacific Coast Hwy. South, page 15.*
Deer Valley Lodge— 2261 Maricopa Hwy., Santa Paula,
(805) 646-4256. *See Santa Paula, page 29.*
Hutchins Route 62 Diner— 55405 29 Palms Hwy., Yucca Valley,
(760) 365-6311. *See Joshua Tree, page 59.*
Las Brisas— 361 Cliff Dr., Laguna Beach, (949) 497-5434.
See Pacific Coast Hwy. South, page 15.
Lavita's— 6105 Carbon Canyon Rd., Brea,
See Pacific Coast Hwy. South, page 15.
Malibu Inn— 22969 Pacific Coast Hwy., Malibu, (310) 456-6106.
See Pacific Coast Hwy. North, page 9.
Johnny McNally's— Moutain 99, Fairview, (760) 376-2430.
See Kern River/ Sherman Pass, page 79.
Newcomb's Ranch— Hwy. 2, Mt. Waterman, Angeles Forest,
(626) 440-1001. *See Angeles Forest/ Big Bear, page 41.*
Wolf Inn— Hwy. 33, about 30 miles northeast of Ojai.
See Santa Paula/ Lockwood Valley, page 29.
Rock Inn— 17539 Lake Elizabeth Rd., Saugus, (805) 724-1855.
See Canyon Country, page 23.
Rock Store— Mullholland Highway, Malibu, (818) 889-1311.
See Mullholland Highway, page 35.
Sagebrush Cantina— 23527 Calabasas Rd., Calabasas, (818) 222-6062.
See Mullholland Highway, page 35.
Swallow's Inn— 31786 Camino Capistrano, Capistrano,
(949) 493-3188. *See Ortega Highway, page 53.*
Walker's Cafe— 700 Paseo Del Mar, San Pedro, (310) 833-3623.
See Pacific Coast Hwy. South, page 15.

HIGHWAY & TOURIST INFORMATION

Road Conditions:
California Highway Patrol Road Information 800-427-7623
Caltrans Highway Information (213) 628-7623

Tourist and Park Bureaus:
Angeles Forest (626) 574-5200

Anza-Borrego (760) 767-5311

Big Bear (909) 866-4601

Death Valley (760) 786-2331

Idyllwild (714) 659-3259

Isabella Lake (760) 379-2742

Laguna Beach (949) 494-1018

National Parks Information Center (818) 597-9192

Palm Springs (800) 967-3767

Ojai (805) 646-8126

San Diego (800) 848-3336

Santa Barbara (800) 927-4688

Santa Monica Mountains (818) 597-9192

Sequoias (209) 565-3341

San Marcos Pass (805) 688-6144

Temecula (909) 676-5090

Ventura (800) 333-2989

FACTORY-AUTHORIZED SOUTHERN CALIFORNIA HARLEY-DAVIDSON DEALERS

Bakersfield
Thorp's Harley-Davidson, Inc.
820-824 18th Street
Bakersfield, CA 93301
(661) 325-3644

Lancaster
Harley-Davidson of Lancaster
45313 23rd Street
Lancaster, CA 93536
(661) 948-5959

Los Angeles Vicinity
Bartels' Harley-Davidson
4141 Lincoln Blvd.
Marina Del Rey, CA 90292
(310) 823-1112

California Harley-Davidson
1517 Pacific Coast Highway
Harbor City, CA 90710
(310) 539-3366

Los Angeles Harley-Davidson
13300 Paramount Blvd.
South Gate, CA 90280
(562) 408-6088

Harley-Davidson of Glendale
3717 San Fernando Road
Glendale, CA 91204
(818) 246-5618

Orange County
Harley-Davidson of Fullerton
2635 W. Orangethorpe
Fullerton, CA 92833
(714) 871-6563

Orange County Harley-Davidson
8677 Research Dr.
Irvine, CA 92618
(949) 727-4464

Harley-Davidson of Westminster
13031 Goldenwest Street
Westminster, CA 92683
(714) 893-6274

Riverside County
Palm Springs Harley-Davidson
19465 N. Indian
N. Palm Springs, CA 92258
(760) 329-1448

Skip Fordyce Harley-Davidson
7840 Indiana Ave.
Riverside, CA 92504
(909) 785-0100

Quaid Temecula Harely-Davidson
28822 Front St.
Temecula, CA 92590
(909) 506-6903

San Bernardino County
Quaid Harley-Davidson
25160 Redlands Blvd.
Loma Linda, CA 92354
(909) 796-8399

Harley-Davidson of Victorville
14522 Valley Center Drive
Victorville, CA 92392
(760) 951-1119

Hutchins Harley-Davidson
55405 29 Palms Highway
Yucca Valley, CA 92284
(760) 365-6311

San Diego County
Harley's House of Harleys
1555 S. Coast Highway
Oceanside, CA 92054
800-4-HARLEY   (619) 433-2060

Harley-Davidson of El Cajon
621 El Cajon Blvd.
El Cajon, CA 92020
(619) 444-1123

South Coast Harley-Davidson
345 E Street
Chula Vista, CA 91910
(619) 420-7000

San Fernando Valley
Barger Harley-Davidson
22107 Sherman Way
Canoga Park, CA 91303
(818) 999-3355

Van Nuys Harley-Davidson
7630 Van Nuys Blvd.
Van Nuys, CA 91405
(818) 989-2230

San Gabriel Valley
Laidlaw's Harley-Davidson
8351 E. Garvey Blvd.
Rosemead, CA 91770
(626) 280-3977

Pomona Valley Harley-Davidson
8710 Central Ave.
Montclair, CA 91763
(909) 981-9500

Santa Maria
Harley-Davidson of Santa Maria
127 E. Main Street
Santa Maria, CA 93454
(805) 928-3668

Ventura
Ventura Harley-Davidson
1326 Del Norte Rd.
Camarillo, CA 93010
(805) 981-9904

Oregon
D&S Harley-Davidson
4526 South Pacific Highway
Phoenix, OR 97535
(541) 535-5515

NO ARTIFICIAL PRESERVATIVES.

When you turn out a new Harley-Davidson® that looks this good, how can you improve its pure, unadulterated beauty? Only with pure, unadulterated Harley-Davidson Genuine Motor Accessories.™ Even for new models like this XL™ 1200C Sportster® Custom,™ we're ready for you. So, just as you'd hoped, you can take your new Harley-Davidson any direction you want. Come in today.

FOR A GENUINE HARLEY-DAVIDSON DEALER NEAR YOU, PLEASE SEE PAGES 92 & 93

WHAT FAT BOYS LIKE
TO DRINK.

Harley-Davidson® motorcycles know what they like. Serve up the drink that was designed for them–Harley-Davidson Genuine™ Motorcycle Oil. A well-oiled Harley-Davidson has a passion for performance and a long life. Serve something else and see how bad a Bad Boy™ can get.

FOR A GENUINE HARLEY-DAVIDSON DEALER NEAR YOU,
PLEASE SEE PAGES 92 & 93